5 GIANTS OF ADVERTISING

Philippe Lorin

with the collaboration of Cristina Alonso

ASSOULINE

5 GIANTS
OF ADVERTISING

© 2001 Assouline Publishing, Inc. for the present edition
First published by Editions Assouline, Paris, France

Assouline Publishing, Inc.
601 West 26th Street
18th floor
New York, NY 10001
USA

www.assouline.com

ISBN: 2 84323 249 X

Translated from the French by Bernard Wooding
Proofreading: Margaret Burnham

Printed in Italy

lasker

he was the man who invented advertising, a hugely important figure. Virtually unknown in Europe, in the United States he is regarded as the father of modern advertising. In fact, few men have done more to change the buying habits of American consumers. His name was Albert Davis Lasker. He left his imprint on many aspects of public life, politics, maritime transportation, merchandising, public relations, civil aviation, Jewish affairs, civil rights, baseball, golf, governments, show business, and philanthropy, in particular medical research. In the realm of advertising alone, his contribution was so prodigious that the results have left an indelible mark on the profession. Lucky Strike, Pepsodent, Kleenex, Palmolive, Kotex, Studebaker, Frigidaire, Sunkist, and RCA are all famous names that were launched and propelled by Lasker. Slogans such as "Keep that schoolgirl complexion" or "Reach for a Lucky instead of a sweet" are classics. Thanks to him, orange juice is now drunk throughout the world. He was an innovator in the merchandising of canned food, powdered milk, and fruit. He encouraged women to smoke and gave them the disposable sanitary pad. One of the first to understand the power of radio, he created soap operas and invented the radio commercial. This man, who left the agency he had bought at the age of twenty when he was sixty-four, was the richest and most influential person in the history of advertising. He made his fortune with nothing but ideas, and yet, despite his importance, he never belonged to an advertising executives' club, never met with his colleagues, never convened a meeting of a board of directors, and never received a client at home unless he was also a friend. All this

Albert Davis Lasker was the father of modern advertising. He became the richest and most influential man in the history of advertising, without ever having published anything and only ever having made six speeches in his whole life.

probably explains why Lasker never became a national figure. He never sought publicity. Nothing was ever written about him in *The New Yorker* and he never made the front cover of *Time* magazine. He was given the shortest of paragraphs in *Who's Who*. He never published anything and made only six speeches during the course of his entire career.

nd yet, although his name is rarely mentioned, the history of advertising would simply not have happened without him. Albert David Lasker was born May 1, 1880, in Freiburg, Germany, into a Jewish family. His family moved to the United States while he was still a child. At age twelve, he single-handedly created a four-page weekly called *The Galveston Free Press*. An annual subscription cost $1, and Albert Lasker made a weekly profit of $15, which was more money than a lot of adults made at the time. He wrote the newspaper himself, mixing editorials that display a wisdom unusual for a twelve-year-old with naïve, poetical observations. Needless to say, he sold advertising, phoning the dentist or the grocer to sell them space. But as owner and editor of the newspaper, he felt it would be undignified to cash the money from the advertising himself, so he appointed an eleven-year-old boy. Naturally, when Lasker entered Ball High School, he became publisher and editor of the school magazine. After a year, he gave up the post because he felt it would be undemocratic to remain in charge for longer. He was very precocious and, by his own admission, organized everything at school. A photograph from the period shows twenty hefty youths in football gear surrounding a slight young man. That young man was the boss, the team coach—Albert Lasker, of course. In 1893, Albert Lasker's father, Morris, abruptly went bankrupt. He had overinvested in real estate and the market had collapsed. Tenants could no longer pay their rent, and Morris Lasker was unable to meet his commitments. His debts rose to $1 million. Morris Lasker sent his wife and children back to Germany, but kept Albert, who

was thirteen, with him. Albert's subsequent loathing of real estate investment dated from this period. Slowly but surely, Morris Lasker resurfaced (he eventually became rich again), and Albert, still at school, started to do the accounting with his father. Furthermore, his precocious talent enabled him to obtain a job on the local daily, *The Galveston Morning News*, covering sports, current events, theater, and business. At the time, 1896,

galveston

was the largest cotton port in the world after Liverpool. Everyone was interested in the price of cotton and its fluctuations, and yet no press association had a regular correspondent in Galveston. Lasker bought a sick correspondent's job from him for $100. This high school student promptly pulled off another remarkable feat, this time as a reporter. At the time, everybody was trying to get in touch with Eugene Debs, the trade union boss who had just been released from prison following his incarceration for organizing a train driver's strike. Lasker tracked him down and disguised himself as a telegraph messenger. When he met Debs, he handed him a false telegram explaining that he was really a young journalist and that, by according him an interview, Debs would be helping him to launch his career. Debs was won over and agreed to do the interview, thereby giving Lasker a scoop. Albert completed his high school studies at the end of this busy year. He was already earning $40 a week. He never went to college. Although he was only seventeen, a future as a journalist seemed all mapped out for him. In his free time, however, Albert had started organizing a boxing club. Only the heavyweights interested him, and he became the manager of one in particular who he called "Dixie Champ." Dixie Champ quickly won a large number of regional bouts, but Lasker had other ideas. He wrote to the reigning champion of the time, Joe Choinsky, and offered him $500 to come to Galveston from Philadelphia to face Dixie Champ. Choinsky agreed, and one fine morning the whole of Galveston turned up at the railroad station to welcome the famous Choinsky. The latter appeared in the doorway of the train and was greeted by the crowd. Dixie Champ looked at the champion's hands—two terrifying paws—and when the train that had brought Choinsky began to depart, he jumped aboard and was never seen again, leaving Lasker in deep trouble. His savings were invested in the fight, his champion had vanished into thin air, and everyone was asking for his money back. Albert suddenly had an idea. He offered an African American by the name of Jack Johnson, who worked for his uncle and who Albert himself had used as a sparring partner for

dixie champ,

$25 to climb into the ring with Choinsky. Johnson accepted. Lasker quickly went to see Choinsky and implored him to let Johnson box for one or two rounds before knocking him out. To everyone's surprise, Johnson, with no faking, lasted four and a half rounds before being knocked out. It was to be the beginning of a career that would take him all the way to a world championship bout. Albert Lasker was still seventeen when his promising career as a journalist took a sharp blow. Among his other duties on the paper, he worked as theater critic. In this capacity he was supposed to attend a performance of *Shore Acres* at the Opera House in Galveston. Unfortunately, he had been chasing a girl from Houston for a while and she had

finally agreed to meet him that same evening. As he knew the play well, Lasker decided to write his article beforehand, arrange to have it delivered to the newspaper during the night, and quickly leave to

An example of the extraordinarily long texts used in advertising at the end of the nineteenth century and the beginning of the twenti-eth. This particular ad was for Winton automobiles.

HOW TO CONTROL A MOTOR CAR IN EMERGENCIES

BY LOYD A. THOMAS

The WINTON of 1905
Vertical, Four-Cylinder Motor.

throw himself into the arms of his lady friend in Houston. The following day, he learned that the Opera House had burned down just before the performance. He didn't even bother to go to the newspaper to collect his paycheck. Instead, he left town, but still with the idea of continuing as a journalist. He subsequently worked for the *Times Democrat* in New Orleans and the *Dallas News*. It was Albert's father who brought his career as a journal-

ist to an end. Albert was intent on heading to the East Coast where the major American newspapers were, but his father was opposed to the idea, because journalists had the reputation of being drunkards. He suggested that Albert go into advertising instead, which he felt would be a worthier trade. Albert was repelled by the idea. For him, it was advertising that was the disreputable activity, not journalism. At this period, writing and advertising were still unconnected activities. Stories were run regardless of whether they might be damaging to advertisers. Eventually, Albert was persuaded to change his mind. To secure him, his father got him a job at Lord & Thomas, following a strange combination of circumstances. In Texas, there was no law relating to bankruptcy, so when somebody went bankrupt he was at liberty to decide which of his creditors he would favor. It was thus possible to come to an agreement with creditor A and completely ignore creditors B, C, and D. Of course, the debtor always tended to favor a member of his own family or a friend. A consortium from the North had come to Galveston to build roads for trol-

This ad by Lord & Thomas, the agency bought by Lasker when he was just twenty-three, was one of the first examples of self-advertising by an ad agency.

9

leys and create housing lots. This consortium had gone bust and owed a large amount of money to Lord & Thomas, who had done the advertising for the project in Chicago. Morris Lasker was instructed by the creditors to represent them. Lord traveled to Galveston, a journey of fifty-two days, because he was owed $30,000, a sum that represented half the company's annual profit.

e met Morris Lasker, who arranged for Lord & Thomas to be one of the favored creditors. Lord told Morris Lasker that he was hugely indebted to him and that he owed him a favor. The latter remembered this promise and had no difficulty getting Albert hired by the advertising agency immediately. Thus in 1889, Albert Lasker, who had just turned eighteen, reluctantly left Galveston to please his father. He intended to remain in Chicago for only a few weeks. He ended up staying in Chicago for forty-four years. The age of modern advertising dawned not because of new economic circumstances, but for a simple, comical reason: during his first month at Lord & Thomas, Albert Lasker lost $500 at craps. At the time he was only paid

ten dollars

a week, much less than he had been making ten years previously in Texas. Nobody paid any attention to him in the agency and he had little to do. Nobody, including himself, expected him to stay there for long. His principal, very prosaic occupation consisted of emptying and cleaning the spittoons, an office accessory that was very popular at the time. With his savings of $75, his weekly salary of $10, and his debts of $500, the young Lasker hadn't gotten off to a good start. Eager for his father not to learn about what was going on, he went to see Mr. Thomas and persuaded him to give him an advance of $500, a fortune at the time. Mr. Thomas went to find the players who had fleeced Lasker and, although he was sure that they had cheated, gave them the money. Of course, Albert had to drop the idea of leaving. He was obliged to stay at the agency, living off $8 a week and paying back $2 a week to the agency. He faced the prospect of 250 weeks of debt, which must have seemed an eternity. He later said that he matured a great deal that day, and he never got into debt again in his life. The following year, one of the employees whose job was to find new clients for the company left. Lasker asked Thomas if he could fill in while they were recruiting a replacement. He was careful not to ask for the $3,500 a week, all expenses paid, that the person he was replacing received, making do with his $10 a week, all expenses paid. On the very first day, he came back with an order for $3,000, although he acknowledged that his predecessor had paved the way for him. The following month, he crisscrossed the Midwest on foot and horseback, by train and car, and even in a sleigh, collecting $50,000 worth of contracts.

n one occasion, in Indiana, he traveled fifteen miles on horseback in the snow to get an account of $300, which left a meager profit of $24. But Lasker also asked Mr. Thomas if he would entrust him with some of the old accounts that weren't doing very well, because they would enable him to gain experience as a copywriter. An opportunity came up in Louisville with the Wilson Ear Drum Company, which made "Common Sense Ear Drums." These were cardboard cones designed to help the hard of hearing. The client only paid the agency 10% and the products were sold by mail at $5 each. Lasker studied the mail order market closely and decided that this type of advertising could be greatly improved. He wrote the advertisement that he thought would work best and, without telling anyone, went to Louisville to show Wilson his advertisement. Wilson was only paying 5% at the time, but Lasker said: "If it pays you, you pay us 15%, and if it doesn't pay you, you quit." Wilson accepted and within two years went from an expenditure of $3,000 on advertising every month to $20,000. Lasker had multiplied the revenue on this account by ten.

The same year, 1899, Lasker pulled off another remarkable achievement. Lord & Thomas learned that the Rheinstrom Brothers in Cincinnati, producers of liqueurs and spirits, had decided to begin advertising with a budget of $10,000. It was said that they had promised their account to the famous Austin Bates in New York. Lasker traveled to Cincinnati. At that time, people worked from 8:00 A.M. to 6:00 P.M., six days a

Men Do Prefer Van Camp's

A Chicago restaurant manager, who serves noon luncheons to hundreds, told us the following facts:

The National Dish **Van Camp's** BAKED WITH TOMATO SAUCE **PORK AND BEANS** The National Dish

Three sizes: 10, 15 and 20 cents per can.

'an Camp Packing Company Established 1861 Indianapolis, Indiana

week, and if you arrived early enough it was easy to identify who was boss, because it was always he who opened the mail, presumably to prevent treachery or espionage on the part of his employees. This was standard practice in many companies at the time, even in large businesses, which were usually run by wealthy men who allowed nobody but themselves to sign checks. Albert Lasker knew this very well.

His train arrived at 7:00 A.M. and he hurried to Rheinstrom's. He waited at the door until the first person arrived for work. At 8:00 A.M., he entered the building and saw a man standing in front of a desk opening the mail. It was the boss, Mr. Abe

Rheinstrom. The latter asked Lasker curtly what he wanted. Lasker handed him his card and explained to him that he worked for Lord & Thomas and that he was coming to ask for his account. Rheinstrom asked him how his company had the gall to send "a kid" like Lasker to bother him early in the morning, when he was busy with the most important work of the day. He told him to get out. Lasker had convinced his employers to let him go to Cincinnati, but he couldn't even get an appointment.

He was certain, however, that Rheinstrom normally went home for lunch. Remembering how he had gotten an interview with Eugene Debs, he called him at

More Mileage from Socks

The *Holeproof Exx Toe* does it, Men!

Now—
3 to 4 times more wear!

**Fine silk socks with wear stopped at most important point.
Cuts expense 60% to 75%! Prices remain 75c and $1.00**

THIS offers you a big saving on silk hosiery for the Summer.

Three to four times more wear than you've ever had before. More than 500 tests prove it will cut hosiery expense 60% to 75%!

Now on sale at all leading men's furnishing shops.

Where silk socks wear out

We wanted to give you silk hosiery that would wear better than anything you've had. We had already given you socks of exceptional style and quality.

So we investigated. Found that 95% of men's hosiery wears out at the toe. Now for years we have experimented to reinforce this point—without making socks bulky, uncomfortable. Today more than 500 tests prove that we have succeeded!

You can't see or feel it

Right at the tip, where your sock comes into contact with the toes, we have put extra reinforcement. You can hardly see or feel it, even on close examination. It can't be felt at all, wearing the hosiery.

But it gives 3 to 4 times more wear than you've ever had before. We made 500 tests to prove this. Now no more mending for your wives and mothers. No more throwing away socks with the uppers still good.

It means a saving of 60% to 75% for you, on hosiery expense.

Today!

We call it the new Holeproof Exx Toe. You can get it, today, in two handsome styles of Holeproof Silk Hosiery for men. Ask for them by number: Style No. 420-Exx, 75c; Style No. 920-Exx, $1.00. If you can't remember the style number, just remember to ask for the Holeproof Exx toe.

At all leading men's furnishing shops. A real way to save money.

Style No. 420-Exx
75c

Style No. 920-Exx
$1.00

On sale at

**Schloss Bros. Co.
L. S. Ayres & Co.
Jud's Men's Duds (3 stores)
Cameron & Schooley
Roberts Clothing Co.**

Holeproof Hosiery

with the new, long-wear *Holeproof Exx Toe*

home and began talking so fast that Rheinstrom could not interrupt him. As a result, Rheinstrom agreed to see him. At the beginning of the century, Lasker was twenty years old. At this time, Battle Creek in Michigan became the scene of fierce competition between the representatives of the different advertising agencies. Two enormous companies making boxed cereals started there:

kellogg,

who made Corn Flakes, and Post, who made Grape Nuts. Relations between the two were not unlike the bitter rivalry between the Capulets and the Montagues. At the time, a number of manufacturers were trying to get rich in the El Dorado of breakfast products. As many as twenty-four companies fought what is usually referred to as the "Battle of Battle Creek." The atmosphere was electric—like Texas during the oil boom. Company shares rose and fell crazily. A company that seemed destined for a brilliant future at midday could be swept away for good by nightfall. When the smoke had cleared, Kellogg and Post were the only survivors, and the two of them went on to change the breakfast habits of Americans for good. Homemade grits and oatmeal gave way to cereals in cardboard cartons. Lasker visited Battle Creek many times. This experience taught him a great deal. He realized that a good product supported by advertising could revolutionize consumer habits throughout the country overnight. Another event attracted Lasker's attention: the formation of the first great American trust, when several hundred cracker manufacturers merged to form the National Biscuit Company. The company was the first advertiser to have an annual advertising budget of $1 million. It was Ayer who got the account and Lasker said to himself: "If Ayer can do it, so can I." Lasker devoted an increasing amount of time to studying copywriting. At Lord & Thomas, one of the largest agencies in the country, there was only one copywriter, and he worked mornings at Lord & Thomas and afternoons at Montgomery Ward, earning

$15 a week from each agency. Similarly, the art department consisted of only one man, who was paid $25 a week. Lasker sensed that this situation would not last, and that the soul of advertising lay in creativity and copywriting. Totally engrossed in his work, he had given up the idea of leaving

lord & thomas

to return to journalism. He himself later confessed that even if he had been given the money to pay off his debt to Mr. Thomas, he still would not have left. What fascinated him most was the mysterious power of advertising. Above all, he wanted to discover the essence of successful advertising by understanding how it worked. While stubbornly seeking an answer to this question, he continued to travel and to sell the agency to new advertisers. At the end of 1900, when Albert was twenty years old, his father, profiting from a trip to Chicago, went to see Lord & Thomas to find out how his son was getting on. Thomas told him that he didn't know whether he was crazy or brilliant, but that he was one or the other, or else both at the same time. In 1901, Albert Lasker visited friends in Cincinnati and met Flora Warner. Although she was already engaged, he decided that she was going be his wife, and indeed he married her in 1902. They settled on the South Side of Chicago, near Midway, a pleasant middle-class neighborhood. Almost as soon as they moved in, Flora fell ill with typhoid fever, which developed into phlebitis and arthritis. She remained an invalid until her death in 1936, although she had three children: Mary in 1904, Edward in 1912, and Frances in 1916. More than ever, Lasker was determined to understand advertising. Always conscious of the enormous power that it exerted and of its newfound efficacy, he wanted to find out exactly what gave it these qualities. But how could you distinguish between good and bad advertising? How could you account for the fact that one campaign increases sales enormously, while another fails to? Lasker began to devote his time

© H. H. Co.

E. M. KLEMPNER

FOR each pretty gown or suit, there's a *style* and *color* in Holeproof Hosiery that's perfectly, exquisitely suited! Sheer —lovely. But with amazing ability to withstand much wear and laundering. In all the newest, most correct colors: Indian Tan, Noisette, Samoan, Caravan, Beige, Cloud, Silver and Jack Rabbit. At most good stores. If not available near you, write for illustrated price list. Styles also for children and men.

Holeproof Hosiery

HOLEPROOF HOSIERY COMPANY
MILWAUKEE, WISCONSIN
Holeproof Hosiery Company of Canada, Limited
London, Ontario

to studying these questions. For this young man of twenty, this quest became a source of anguish and even torture. He begged the old hands to teach him, to reveal the secret of advertising. But nobody knew any more than he did; nobody was able to give him a convincing answer. For a while, he clung to the idea that advertising was information, but then how could you explain the fact that some advertisements contained lots of information and were flops? He made a systematic analysis of the slogans of other advertising agencies. Lord & Thomas's was "Advertise Judiciously," but Lord & Thomas were incapable of saying what was meant by the word "judiciously." Spend more wisely? Write better advertisements? Ayer's slogan didn't satisfy him either: "Keeping Everlastingly At It Brings Success." "Supposing I start wrong and I keep everlastingly at it?" asked Lasker. "Where is that going to get me?" He asked an Ayer employee, "What is right in advertising?" and

the man replied, "Keeping your name before the people." Lasker objected, with justification: "Supposing I can't live that long. Supposing I go broke, that I can't keep my name before the people. There must be something else to this thing." The year 1903 was a turning point in Albert Lasker's life. At the age of twenty-three, he took control of Lord & Thomas, a company he would own and rule with an iron hand for forty-four years. Daniel M. Lord retired at the age of sixty, as he always said he would, and Lasker, who had saved a large sum of money thanks to his prospecting bonuses, bought Lord's shares. In an instant, his annual salary rose to $52,000, probably the highest salary in the United States for someone of his age. Shortly after, in the spring of 1904, the famous answer he had sought arrived in an

Ads were becoming more refined in style, despite the deliberate absence of graphic design. The use of typography was becoming more sophisticated and the layout was evolving. Copywriting was already an important part of advertising by this time, thanks to its inventor—Lasker.

unexpected way. He was in the same office as Mr. Thomas when an employee bought the latter a note. Thomas read it and handed it to Lasker. It said: "I am in the saloon downstairs. I can tell you what advertising is. I know you don't know. It will mean much to me to have you know what it is and it will mean much to you. If you wish to know what advertising is, send the word 'yes' down by the bellboy." It was signed John E. Kennedy. Thomas asked Lasker: "Did you ever hear of such a name?" Lasker had never heard of him. Thomas decided that he must be crazy and that he didn't have any time to waste. Lasker said: "Let me see him. What do we have to lose?" Kennedy met with Lasker; their meeting lasted until midnight. Lasker now knew what advertising was–Kennedy had given him the correct formula in three words:

salesmanship in print.

Today, this definition might seem obvious or simplistic and, of course, incomplete, but at the time nobody had summed up the concept in such simple terms. These three words have defined advertising ever since, even though the word "print" has been augmented and enriched by radio and television. Lasker, of course, wanted Kennedy to join Lord & Thomas. He spoke about it to Thomas, who had not only never paid a copywriter more than $30 a week, but in addition developed an aversion to Kennedy. Nevertheless, he realized that it might be good for the agency and agreed, on condition that he never had to deal with Kennedy. So the latter entered the company on the fabulous salary of $28,000 a year. Lasker and Kennedy immediately began to work together at a feverish pace. Two years later, Kennedy was receiving $75,000 a year, and Lasker decided that Lord & Thomas should be the first agency to have a team of copywriters. He revealed his plan to Thomas: "I have been upstairs and I have measured that if we take out all the files against the north windows and all the files against half of the west windows, we can make nine offices, eight by ten each, that will cost around $2,000 to build, and advertise for nine young newspaper men. I will train them with Kennedy, and maybe out of the nine we'll keep three or four." Thomas agreed. Lord & Thomas thus became the first agency in the world, under the impetus of Lasker, to systematically train young people to become copywriters.

ennedy subsequently left the agency to set up on his own in New York; nobody knows what became of him. But Lasker, the great innovator, had an unrivaled talent for finding men and training them. Nobody, except perhaps Rubicam, would be able to do this so successfully. By 1905, Lasker was in charge of copywriting at the agency. By this time, he had stopped writing himself, but was full of ideas and supplied the creative spark for all the agency's work. In 1906, Mr. Thomas had a heart attack in the street and died in the arms of Albert Lasker. Lasker, along with Charles Erwin, who would later found the agency Erwin Wasey, bought up Thomas's shares. Although he was the majority shareholder by far, Lasker still bought Erwin's stake six years later. Year after year, business grew. Lasker threw himself headlong into his work, sacrificing his private life, his leisure time, and his interests outside advertising, so strong was his belief in his clients' products, and, of course, in advertising. He was now a man, a tall man for his period and slender. His physical energy consumed everything he absorbed. Always moving, tense, combative, very animated, passionately in love with life, he was full of curiosity and developed childish passions for things. He was radiant. He always addressed his colleagues by their surnames, preceded by Mr. or Mrs., even those he had known from the beginning. He would have nothing to do with the fake camaraderie prevalent in the advertising world. Similarly, nobody ever called him Al or Bert. To everyone, he was Mr. Lasker. Throughout his life, he was easily upset. He was prone to the most extreme forms of behavior according to the mood

he was in. If things looked bleak, he was so emotional that he made them out to be even bleaker. His first wife, Flora, recalled that on one occasion she went to meet him at the train station after a business trip. He had lost a large account. He got off the train looking pale and dejected. "I am ruined. We are poor," he said. He said that he had to go to the office urgently. Flora pointed out that if they were ruined, there was no need for him to go to the office and that he would be better off going home to have breakfast. In 1908, the legendary Claude Hopkins, author of *Scientific Advertising*, came into Lasker's life. Like Lasker, Hopkins had never gone to college. He had started earning his living at the age of nine, spending several years as a church cleaner. Like Lasker, he was a tireless worker and for many years never left his office before 2:00 A.M. His favorite day was Sunday, because he could work all day without being interrupted. Thus, after thirty-five years in the advertising business, he was able to claim that he had in fact worked for sixty-five years, since he got through two years' work in the space of one year. Unlike Lasker, he was stingy and always refused to pay more than $6.50 for a pair of shoes. Hopkins had his first successes when he was still a teenager and was working at Bissell, a carpet-sweeper company. He brought about a minor revolution by creating a range of bright colors, obliging retailers to keep every color in stock. His most remarkable feat occurred at the beginning of the 1900s, when he was in charge of advertising at Shwift and Co. One of Shwift's products was called

cotosuet.

This replacement for butter or bacon fat, made from lotus seed oil and beef fat, had a competitor, Cottolene, which was better distributed. Hopkins' challenge was to beat Cottolene—a challenge which was about as easy as launching a new white soap against Ivory, the most popular soap in America. Hopkins learned that a famous Chicago department store was going to open a new branch and would be celebrat-

Live Your Romances!

Keep That Schoolgirl Complexion!

**In Paris, too,
It's now Palmolive**

Today in France, home of cosmetics, Palmolive is one of the two largest selling toilet soaps, having supplanted French soaps by the score. French women, the most sophisticated of all women in beauty culture, by the thousands have discarded French soaps and adopted safe and gentle Palmolive.

Retail Price
10ᶜ *Palmolive Soap is untouched by human hands until you break the wrapper—it is never sold unwrapped*

*B*EAUTY, *Charm, Youth* may not be the fundamentals of Romance, but they *help*. Few readers of a "best seller" picture the heroine more than partially unpossessed, at least, of those attributes.

To *live* one's romances today, one stays young as long as she can, makes herself as *naturally attractive* as she can and trusts the rest to her womanly intelligence. Under modern rules in skin care, thousands of women have gone an amazingly long way in that direction.

Those rules, say experts, start with cleansing the skin *regularly* of beauty-imperiling accumulations; which means the use of soap and water. The only secret is in *What Kind of Soap* one uses. Only a true complexion soap should ever be used on the face.

Do this night and morning

So, largely on expert advice, more and more thousands of women turn to the balmy lather of Palmolive, used this way:

Wash your face gently with soothing Palmolive Soap, massaging the lather softly into the skin. Rinse thoroughly, first with warm water, then with cold.

If your skin is inclined to be dry, apply a touch of good cold cream—that is all. Do this regularly, and particularly in the evening.

Use powder and rouge if you wish. But never leave them on over night. They clog the pores, often enlarge them. Blackheads and disfigurements often follow. They must be washed away.

Avoid this mistake

Do not use ordinary soaps in the treatment given above. Do not think any green soap, or one represented as of olive and palm oils, is the same as Palmolive.

And it costs but 10c the cake! So little that millions let it do for their bodies what it does for their faces. Obtain a cake—then note the difference one week makes. The Palmolive-Peet Co., Chicago. Ill.

KEEP THAT SCHOOLGIRL COMPLEXION

ing the event. The grocery department, located on the fifth floor, had a large bay window. Hopkins asked if he could use this bay window, promising to do the best advertising for the store. He then asked a baker to make an enormous cake, made with Cotosuet and not with butter. The cake occupied the entire bay, was almost as tall as the window, and was wonderfully decorated. All that was left for Hopkins to do was to create his advertisements talking about the cake and Cotosuet. This action caused a sensation. Police had to stop people from throwing themselves on the cake. In the space of a few days, 105,000 people climbed the five flights to see the famous cake. To top it all, Hopkins organized a competition, which involved guessing the weight of the cake, and to take part you had to bring a Cotosuet wrapper. However, it was another advertisement that put Lasker onto Hopkins' track: a

Schlitz advertisement with the slogan "Poor Beer VS Pure Beer." One day, Lasker was traveling by train with Cyrus Curtis, the owner of the press group of the same name. Curtis told Lasker that he was going to order a bottle of Schlitz because of an advertisement that he had read, and that Lasker should get hold of the person who wrote it. Lasker was disconcerted because Curtis never drank alcohol. He even banned articles on alcoholic beverages from his magazines, and yet here he was drinking a beer because of an advertisement that talked of its purity. Lasker got hold of the name of the copywriter who wrote it: Hopkins. But how could he get him to join Lord & Thomas? Hopkins was already rich and was tired of working. Lasker went to see a friend who knew Hopkins well. This person told him that he would not be able to tempt Hopkins by offering him money, but that he might succeed by giving his wife an electric automobile. She dreamed of owning one, but was the victim of her husband's usual cheapness. It was quickly done, and Hopkins joined Lord & Thomas, earning $185,000 a year. He stayed with them for eighteen years, until he retired in 1924. Under the management of Albert Lasker, who was not yet thirty years old, Lord & Thomas overtook Ayer & Thomson, becoming the biggest agency in the world. One of the clients acquired by the agency was Sunkist. They were one of Lasker's favorite clients, a fondness which dated to a period when he regarded it as criminal to cut down orange trees, wasting natural resources. His idea was revolutionary: to persuade the public to drink orange juice. At the time, people ate oranges but did not drink juice. The sales of

sunkist

grew at a staggering rate, and the producers were no longer forced to cut down their trees. This is a perfect example of the way in which, from the earliest days of advertising, a simple idea coupled with a well-developed campaign can save an industry, lead to the creation of a new one, and bring about a radical change in the behavior of the public. In 1911, another important client, Palmolive, joined Lord & Thomas. A soap manufacturer from Milwaukee, BP Johnson and Co., asked Lasker to look after one of its products: Galvanic Laundry Soap. Lasker refused because he felt that he couldn't do anything for the product, and asked Charles Pearce, the sales manager, if he had another product to entrust to him. Pearce told him that they manufactured a toilet soap called "Palmolive," the first green soap in the world, but its sales were so marginal that it was not worth pushing them. Immediately, Lasker's interest was aroused. Why was it green? Why was it called Palmolive? Pearce told him that the soap contained palm oil and olive oil. Lasker had an idea for a revolutionary advertisement: responding to its exotic, cosmetic appearance rather than its cleansing properties, he decided that Palmolive would be a beauty product for the modern woman. The rest is history. Beauty soap advertising was born. Within a few years,

palmolive

would be the best-selling soap in the world. In addition, Lasker inaugurated the coupon technique with Palmolive, making it possible to obtain a small sample of the soap to try. The best-known Palmolive slogan, "Keep that schoolgirl complexion," would be translated or adapted throughout the world.

In the same period, Lord & Thomas acquired new accounts, generated by the new automobile industry. But Lasker was not enthusiastic, preferring consumer goods such as cigarettes and electrical appliances. The age of the automobile was in its infancy and, in 1910, there were only 1,200 miles of tarmac road throughout the entire United States. Although most automobile manufacturers felt that advertising served no purpose, Lord & Thomas presented itself as a pioneer. Lasker's first client in this sector was John Willis, who created Willis Overland. He had no money, and Lasker offered to advance him $200,000,

just to prove to him that advertising

worked. Willis accepted, and Lasker

gave the *Saturday Evening Post* the first

double-page ad in history other than

the center spread, with a heading and

a highly detailed text. Willis's sales

rocketed. Lord & Thomas went on to

work for Hudson, Chalmers, and

R.E.O. (the initials of R. E. Olds,

which became Oldsmobile).

asker also dealt with Goodyear, which started with a budget of $40,000 and quickly rose to $2 million. Lasker could not bear the idea of creating demand for a brand of tire, knowing that this demand would not be satisfied because the brand was not known to distributors. He therefore offered to put retailers' names in local advertisements, providing they had $250 worth of Goodyear tires in stock. Some 30,000 retailers accepted. This was yet another example of a new type of advertisement created by Lasker. A little later, Albert Lasker invested $1 million in a new manufacturer, Mitchell, but lost all the money in one year. Put off by this bad experience, when he had the opportunity of taking over Maxwell soon after, he refused point blank. A young man by the name of Walter P. Chrysler bought the company, and everyone knows what happened next. Lasker did make a contribution to the automobile industry when he had the idea, with Albert Erskine, the president of Studebaker, for a four-door model. This was at the beginning of World War I. Lord & Thomas by that time had branches in Los Angeles, San Francisco, New York, Toronto, London, and even Paris. This enormous success was due not only to Lasker's tal-

ent, but also to the advent of mass production and consumption, and the growth of leisure activities. The automobile, the airplane, and the radio all became part of everyday life. In this new world, Lasker headed the field. He was the starting point for every innovation. Lord & Thomas, nicknamed the "Cheltenham Bold agency" because of the typeface that Lasker insisted on for all the agency's advertisements, trained and had the best copywriters. People used to joke: "If someone is fired from Lord & Thomas, he can get a job anywhere." In 1916, nine of the most important American agencies were managed by former Lord & Thomas employees. Clients were accepted or refused by Lasker. To be accepted was like having one's son admitted to Harvard. Thanks to Lasker, advertising became active instead of being a simple reminder, and for twenty-five years he was the man who contributed most to the expansion of business in America and the growing importance of mass distribution in the American way of life. However, Lasker had a kind of mental block in two areas: market research and art directors. He hated studies and refused to have an art department. Certain of the power of copywriting, Lasker didn't hire his first art director until much later, when he felt that his ads would be more effective if they were illustrated. When they did eventually start to use illustrations, Lord & Thomas made record profits: although lacking a research department or an art department, the agency achieved 7% or 8% profit, when most agencies struggled to reach 3% (today, agencies struggle to reach 1%). Lasker was by this time paying himself an income of $1 million a year. He had always been unconcerned by the way he dressed. Too busy to go shopping for clothes, he entrusted the task to his valet, who was about the same size and used to go to the tailor for him. That was how Lasker gradually came to wear jackets with bold checks and flamboyant ties. The explanation was simple: Lasker always gave his valet his used clothes, so the latter would choose what he liked. In 1940, when Lasker married his second wife, Marie Reinhart, she gave his clothing a serious overhaul, and he subsequently appeared on the list of the ten best-dressed men in America. Sensitive, perceptive, impassioned even, his approach to everything, including money, was romantic. Like all true romantics, he sometimes seemed to be disenchanted, but could equally easily develop intense enthusiasm for some new company, preferably foolish and high-risk. It goes without saying that as soon as his projects were put into practice, he grew bored and abruptly discarded them for his next interest. He used

humor as a weapon,

a tool, and remembered an incredible number of funny stories, which he would bring out at the right moment—usually when it was necessary to take the tension out of a situation. Beyond his sense of humor, he was able to see the funny side of things. These qualities enabled him to make a big impact on people, who sought his company in growing numbers. He was not cynical, but changed his mind about things through conviction. A fervent Republican for many years, he ended up voting for Franklin D. Roosevelt and Harry Truman. An ardent isolationist, opposed to the United States joining NATO, he became a disciple of Wendell Wilkie (the Democrat defender of the NATO project) and fervent advocate of the "One World" idea of international cooperation (Atlantic Pact). He who hated graphic art put together, at the age of sixty, one of the most remarkable collections of paint-

A rather clumsy attempt to give Palmolive, a soap invented about 1910 by Johnson & Co., some roots. They quickly returned to the slogan "That Schoolgirl Complexion."

ings in the world. Always intrigued by new things, he remained an adolescent to the end. In 1912, still a fairly young man, Lasker had a house built on the edge of the Lake Shore Country Club in Glencoe. He had chosen this place for several reasons: the Lake Shore Country Club was Jewish (other clubs usually only accepted gentiles); he liked to live near his friends; and he enjoyed playing poker. Lasker commissioned Samuel Marx to design his house. Marx had studied in Paris and was one of the most sophisticated architects in the Midwest. But their friendship came to an end after a comical incident. At 2:00 A.M. one night, Lasker was awaken by a noise in his bedroom and saw that there was a leak in the ceiling. He called Marx and asked him to come immediately. Marx, furious at being awakened at 2:00 A.M., asked him how big the hole was. "The size of a pencil," said Lasker. "Well," said Marx, in a typical reply, "put a pencil in it and I'll come round tomorrow." Lasker never spoke to him again. Lasker was working harder than ever at this time, arriving at the office at 7:30 A.M. and returning home after midnight. He was obsessed with being close shaven, to the point almost of bleeding. It was the beginning of a serious depression. If he had to speak for more than five minutes, he would start to sob. He was thirty-two years old at the beginning of World War I, an event which triggered a period of dramatic modernization in the United States, symbolized by the Ford Model T and the equally famous Kleenex. The main protagonist in the Kotex-Kleenex affair was Albert Lasker, of course. This saga can be traced back to two events. In 1878, four young entrepreneurs created

a paper factory at Neenah, Wisconsin, in the heart of the Menowinie Native

American reservation. The company that took the name Kimberly, Clark and Co.,

is still famous today, since it supplied paper for, among other clients, *The New York*

Times and *The New Yorker*. Another important person, F.J. Sensenbrenner, the son

of a blacksmith in Neenah who had left school at fourteen, became the accountant

at Kimberly & Clark Company (as it was now called) in 1899 and rose through the

Naturally Lovable

"That Schoolgirl Complexion"

—is kept and safeguarded by thousands through
following this simple rule in daily skin care

MODERN beauty culture, today, starts largely with choosing a bland complexion soap.

That's the reason millions use Palmolive —a soap made solely to safeguard the skin. In America, it is the largest selling toilet soap. In France, it is one of the two largest - the "imported" soap in beauty-wise Paris, that is supplanting French soaps by the score!

AS more women become skilled in the ways of beauty, more and more turn to natural ways in skin care.

That means a clean skin; pores kept free of accumulations to perform their functions *naturally*.

Thus modern beauty culture starts with soap and water; its only secret being the KIND of SOAP one uses—and how.

Palmolive is a beauty soap. A soap made of bland and soothing cosmetic oils, solely for one purpose; to safeguard the complexion. A soap made to be used freely, lavishly on the skin.

Used in the following way, it is credited with more beautiful skins, probably, than any other beauty method. Its results you see on every side today.

The rule to follow if guarding a good complexion is your goal

Wash your face gently with soothing Palmolive

Soap, massaging the lather softly into the skin. Rinse thoroughly, first with warm water, then with cold. If your skin is inclined to be dry, apply a touch of good cold cream—that is all. Do this regularly, and particularly in the evening. Use powder and rouge if you wish. But never leave them on over night. They clog the pores, often enlarge them. Blackheads and disfigurements often follow. They must be washed away.

Avoid this mistake

Do not use ordinary soaps in the treatment given above. Do not think any green soap, or one represented as of olive and palm oils, is the same as Palmolive.

And it costs but 10c the cake! So little that millions let it do for their bodies what it does for their faces. Obtain a cake today. Then note the amazing difference one week makes. The Palmolive Company (Del. Corp.), Chicago, Ill.

Retail
Price
3484

10c *Palmolive Soap is untouched by human hands until you break the wrapper—it is never sold unwrapped*

KEEP THAT SCHOOLGIRL COMPLEXION

ranks to become president. That was how the Kleenex side of the saga started. It all dated back to 1887, when Ernst Mahler was born in Vienna. When he was old enough, Mahler decided he would work at his father's paper factory and studied the chemistry of cellulose at the Darmstadt technical college. In the end, however, he was hired by a large technical consortium to give his opinion on the paper offcuts used for magazines. Kimberly & Clark, who only employed one full-time chemist at the time, were very impressed by Mahler's knowledge, and he was offered a job. It was the beginning of a great partnership, which would last a long time. During World War I,

mahler

invented the substance that was to become Kotex, the famous disposable sanitary pad. At the time, there was a shortage of cotton throughout America and a substitute was desperately being sought to make bandages, dressings, and surgical supplies for the American troops fighting in Europe. While working on cellulose, Mahler invented a spongy, absorbent, aerated composite that proved satisfactory. Kimberly & Clark patented it under the name Cellucotton. Large quantities were dispatched to the army, the Red Cross, and military hospitals. Suddenly a rumor began to go around that nurses were using these new substances not only as dressings for the wounded, but also for themselves as sanitary pads. A few nurses who were asked confirmed that the product was very suitable and suggested a few modifications. Although Mahler had never thought of this use, he agreed with his colleagues at Kimberly & Clark to take advantage of this opportunity. The new product was christened

and was launched around 1921. However, despite the fact that Kotex clearly met a need and saved thousands of women laundry expenses, the product hardly sold at all. Menstruation was a taboo subject; women were ashamed to go into a drugstore and ask openly for Kotex. The company hired an advertising agency, but sales remained stagnant. The advertisements were not bad, but the message was necessarily indirect. The advertisements had to get people to guess what Kotex was used for, because no magazine would accept an advertisement using the term "sanitary pad" and even less the word "menstruation." Then Lasker arrived on the scene. Kotex had just made it known that it was looking for an advertising agency. Lasker went to see them and was received by Mahler in person. Mahler

explained his problem calmly. Lasker became very excited. For him, Kotex represented an important advance for women, and he was determined to make it an industrial and commercial success. Mahler asked Lasker if hygiene was the only reason that he appeared to be so interested. Lasker enthusiastically replied that the advertising he liked doing most was for products that are only used once. Lasker the idealist and Lasker the businessman were united, and Mahler was convinced.

hen tackling the Kotex problem, Lasker worked with his usual energy. He convinced the magazines to accept a more direct advertisement, assuring them that they would be tactful. He convinced Kimberly & Clark to wrap all the packets of Kotex in white paper. He persuaded retailers to place the

"Mr. Lasker, do you like putting germs in your pocket?" That was how Ernst Mahler presented Kleenex to Lasker.

packets in a pile on the counter, accompanied by a box. Thus women would not have to ask anything of anyone. All they would need to do was to put 50¢ in the box and help themselves. All this he also announced in advertisements. In addition, he persuaded several magazines, including his friend Curtis's *Ladies' Home Journal,* to publish an article on menstruation and to organize an information campaign in schools. Kotex became a success, and one that Lasker was enormously proud of. About 1924,

kleenex

appeared. This was also one of Mahler's inventions. Suffering from hay fever, he explored the idea of creating a cellulose-type tissue that could be used as a handkerchief. He managed to develop a product, calling it "Celluwipes." It was renamed Kleenex' Kerchiefs. Mahler presented the product to Lasker, who seemed skeptical. "It's fine for getting makeup off, but as a handkerchief it's useless." Mahler replied, "Mr. Lasker, do you like putting germs in your pocket?" This reply instantly changed Lasker's view, and he launched a campaign along the lines of the handkerchief that you can throw away, suggesting that a handkerchief full of germs is a menace for everyone. The handkerchief industry protested, but the campaign went ahead and Kleenex was an instant success. Lasker insisted that the tissue be made larger and that they create the famous box that they are still sold in today. A short while later, Lasker invested $3.5 million in Kimberly & Clark shares. Another adventure Lasker was involved in was Pepsodent. What fascinated him most of all was discovering a new market. During World War I, hundreds of thousands of Americans who had never seen a toothbrush in their lives were required by the army to learn to brush their teeth. Thus, there was clearly an opening, a big opening, for a good, reasonably priced toothpaste. Pepsodent was launched by Douglas Smith, the principal owner of Liquozone, a multipurpose medicine. This product

"Amazing—so many women must learn this from others"

—writes a Washington hostess

The embarrassment of this grave social offense is finally ended. This scièntific sanitary pad is now treated by patented* process to end all offense.

WHERE smart women gather socially—or in business—even the most attractive are guilty of offending others at certain times. Yet they, themselves, seldom realize it. When told, they become miserably self conscious. They try in vain to overcome the difficulty by make-shift methods. Now science offers safe and certain relief from this fear.

Kotex now scientifically deodorizes*

Millions of women have learned to depend on Kotex within the last ten years. It has brought them better health, greater peace-of-mind under trying conditions. Now comes an added advantage. Kotex chemists have discovered (and patented) a process that absolutely ends all odors. After several years of research, the one remaining problem in connection with sanitary pads is solved!

No more bulky outlines

That awful feeling of being conspicuous because of the bulkiness of old-time methods is gone, too. Kotex pads are rounded and tapered so there is no evidence of sanitary protection when worn. You may add or remove layers of filler, as needed—a thing all women appreciate. There is a new softness, because both filler and gauze have been specially treated. Finally, Kotex is so easy to dispose of, eliminating all need of laundering.

Buy a box today, at any drug, dry goods or department store . . . 45c for a box of twelve. Supplied, also, in rest-room vending cabinets.

*Kotex is the only sanitary pad that deodorizes by a patented process. (Patent No. 1,670,587, granted May 22, 1928.)

Deodorizes . . . *and 4 other important features:*

1 — *Softer gauze* ends chafing; pliable filler absorbs as no other substance can:

2 — *Corners are rounded* and tapered; no evidence of sanitary protection under any gown;

3 — *Deodorizes*—safely, thoroughly, by a new and exclusive patented process:

4 — *Adjust it to your needs;* filler may be made thinner, thicker, narrower as required;
and

5 — *It is easily disposed of;* no unpleasant laundry.

KOTEX

The New Sanitary Pad which deodorizes

was regarded as old-fashioned and was criticized by the press. Smith had to come up with something new. One day, suffering from a painful toothache, he went to see his dentist, who told him that he had developed a new toothpaste formula that was effective against plaque. Smith bought the formula and Pepsodent was born. One of Smith's partners was Louis Eckstein, who was also a shareholder in publishing, real estate, and pharmaceutical companies. Eckstein was a neighbor of Lasker's and the two men were friends. It was therefore not surprising that when Eckstein became involved with Pepsodent, Lasker should also become interested. Pepsodent had been on the market for four years when Lasker made it a success in 1916. When the product was explained to him, he recommended banishing for good the word "plaque" from advertisements and replacing it by the term "film."

pepsodent

thus was positioned as a toothpaste that rid teeth of their film. When a new substance was later added to Pepsodent's initial formula, Lasker, highly excited, asked what sort of detergent was used. He was told that it was sodium alcyl sulfate. He decided that this would be too technical to be used in advertisements and that another name would have to be found. He even insisted that it should have three vowels and two consonants. The name "irium" was chosen and made Pepsodent a great success. But until the day he died, Lasker never had the remotest idea what irium might be, apart from the fact that it cleaned teeth well. He liked to joke about this: "I invented irium," he would say, "now tell me what it is." What fascinated Lasker about Pepsodent was that the product sold without any need for salesmen. It was the first consumer product that did not use a sales representative or agent, thereby offering Lasker a clear demonstration of the efficacy of advertising. About 1928, Lasker became one of the biggest shareholders in Pepsodent. In the 1920s, Lasker was still making more money than everyone else, but had lost his status as leader that he acquired before World War I. Lord & Thomas made $14 million in business transacted, Ayer $17 million, and J. Walter Thomson $22 million. But Lasker achieved these results with only thirty-six clients, as against fifty-five for J. Walter Thomson and seventy for Ayer. In the 1920s, Lord & Thomas acquired the biggest account in its history: the American Tobacco Company and its Lucky Strike brand.

his advertiser represented as much as all the agency's other clients put together. Lord & Thomas's business doubled and then tripled. Lucky Strike remained Lasker's biggest account for fifteen years. After World War I, sales of ready-made cigarettes boomed in America. Previously, they had been regarded as effeminate; real men, tough guys, used to chew tobacco or smoke a pipe or cigar. If they smoked cigarettes, they would roll them. Faced with the surge in demand for ready-made cigarettes, manufacturers developed the first blends, mainly of Virginia and Turkish tobaccos. Reynolds created Camel, Ligget and Myers created Chesterfield, while American Tobacco had fallen a little behind in the race. The company was spreading its efforts across nearly fifty brands of tobacco, cigars, and cigarettes. Each of these brands had its own small budget and none of them managed to make much of an impact. At the time,

lucky strike

was the name of a chewing tobacco, not a cigarette. To compete with Camel and Chesterfield, American Tobacco decided to create a new blend for cigarettes, giving it the name "Lucky Strike," which was well-known and had a good image. The packet itself was identical to that of the chewing tobacco—green and red. Lucky Strike enjoyed modest success. Then Lasker became involved and made Lucky Strike an unprecedented success. The Lord & Thomas office in New York had done

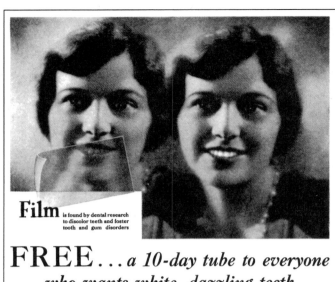

good business before the war, but had subsequently struggled. One day, the agency

was visited by a colleague, Lou Hartman, who had previously had some success

with the launch of Blue Boar, one of American Tobacco's small brands. Hartman

knew the president, Percival Hill, as well as his son, George Washington Hill, who

was in charge of advertising. Lasker traveled to New York to have lunch with Hill

senior and junior. Lasker explained to them that if they continued to spread their

resources across a large number of small brands, they would never be able to catch

up with Camel and Chesterfield. He recommended that they stop all advertising for

the other brands and put the entire budget into Lucky Strike. By the end of lunch,

Lasker was in charge of Lucky Strike. Lasker then asked

percival hill

who was in charge of advertising. Mr. Hill senior replied that it was his son. Lasker

insisted that George come to Chicago for a week to watch how the agency worked.

If he liked what he saw, then he could ask Lord & Thomas to handle the account. Percival Hill died two years later, in 1925, and the lives of Lasker and George Washington Hill became inter-linked for many years to come. The son was forty at the time, five years younger than Lasker, and was a strange man. Relations with Lasker reached a breaking point on several occasions because of their violent disagree-ments and the clash of two enormous egos. After years of being bullied and ordered around by his father, George Washington Hill at last had the chance to assert himself—and assert himself he did! He was a small man who dressed like a cowboy. He wore a large-rimmed hat that he kept clamped to his head at all times, even when working at the office. This hat was his crown, a symbol of his power, and was decorated with hooks and floats because he was crazy about fishing. He loved driving down Fifth Avenue in his Cadillac convertible with a bodyguard standing at the back, the windshield surrounded by packets of Lucky Strike. He owned a house on Manhattan's smart East Side, but spent most of his time in his mansion in Irvingstone, New Jersey, with his two hunting dogs Mr. Lucky and Mrs. Strike. An excellent businessman, he took American Tobacco's sales from $153 million to $558 million in less than twenty years. He ran the company sin-gle-handedly in a strict but nevertheless capricious way. He was capable, for example, of hiring two public relations consultants without either being made

In 1916, Douglas Smith, the owner of Liquozone, bought from a dentist a formula for a tooth-paste that was very effective against plaque.

aware of the situation, simply to deprive his competitors of their services. His motto could have been "I am the king." Needless to say, Hill was a very difficult person. Outside of fishing, but to a much lesser degree, his only interest in life was Lucky Strike, and that interest was not in manufacturing, only sales. That was all he lived for. Evidently, when Lasker and Hill worked together, sparks flew. The room wasn't big enough for two such larger-than-life figures, but Lasker always managed to cope once he had found out how to handle him. His method was to let Hill act as if he was the advertising agency and he, Lasker, was the client. Yet it was Lasker rather than Hill who made Lucky Strike a success. When Lord & Thomas took on the account, Camel sold 100 million cigarettes a day, Chesterfield 60 million, and Lucky Strike only 25 million. Three years later, Lucky Strike was selling 150 million cigarettes a day; it would be the market leader for twenty years. Lasker's first move for Lucky Strike was the most brilliant stroke of all. At the time, it was very unusual for women to smoke and impossible for them to smoke in public. The most that could be done in advertising had been to show a man smoking and a woman saying: "I love the smell of a good cigarette." Lasker's thinking was simple: if we can get

women

to smoke, we will double our market. One day, Lasker was lunching with his wife Flora in a famous restaurant in Chicago. Flora had put on quite a lot of weight and, odd though it might seem today, the doctor had advised her to smoke a cigarette before meals to calm her nerves and improve digestion. So she lit a cigarette. The restaurant manager, horrified, rushed to them, and obsequiously remarked to Lasker that he could not allow his wife to smoke in public. He suggested that they have their meal in a small private room. Lasker was furious. He felt it was intolerable that a woman was not allowed to smoke in a restaurant and was more than ever determined that women should be allowed to smoke in public. In fact, attitudes changed quickly. European women, who were much admired by their American counterparts, in particular actresses and opera singers, smoked in public and Lasker saw this as the perfect argument for abolishing this taboo in America. He devised a campaign that would have no chance of existing today. He pictured celebrities saying: "Lucky Strikes are soothing for the throat," or, more incredibly, "I protect my precious voice thanks to Lucky Strike." Very soon, the most famous voices from the Metropolitan Opera were offering their services free. And then, talkies having just revolutionized the movies, Lasker developed the campaign by using the new screen stars.

he success was incredible. Throughout the country, women began to smoke–Lucky Strikes to begin with, of course. Some time later, while on a trip to Pittsburgh, Lasker learned that a group of candy manufacturers were preparing a campaign to counter the cigarette advertisements. This was not a moral combat against cigarettes. It was simply that people were spending more and more money on cigarettes and less and less on candy. Candy manufacturers thus allocated $150,000 for a campaign, saying that sucking a candy curbed the need to smoke. When he heard this news, Lasker had a mischievous idea. Everyone, he said, is afraid of growing fat and candy makes you fat. Why not organize a campaign proclaiming that it would be best to avoid eating candy and smoke cigarettes instead, since cigarettes do not make you fat and curb the desire for candy? Lasker hurried to New York to tell Hill his idea, but before he could open his mouth Hill outlined exactly the same idea, which had come to him following a discussion in Paris with a woman in her sixties who pretended to be in her forties. She smoked, but never touched candy. The campaign was immediately centered on the theme: "Reach for a Lucky instead of a sweet." The campaign led to a 312% increase in sales. On another occasion,

George Washington Hill invited Albert Lasker to attend a tobacco auction with him. At the end of the auction, Lasker noticed that the floor was littered with crumpled cigarette packets and he carefully calculated the ratio of Lucky Strikes to other brands. Eight days later, an advertisement appeared with a magnificent illustration showing an auction of the period with the farmers and tobacco planters raising their hands to push up the bidding. The heading was based on a simple observation: "Four out of five tobacco planters smoke Lucky Strike." During its collaboration with Lord & Thomas, Lucky Strike spent $180 million on advertising. Lasker always maintained that what drove advertisers to drink, gave them ulcers, or made them depressed was basically the fact that they had to promote products that they despised, or at the very least didn't believe in. The attention that Lasker devoted to the

products

handled by the agency became obsessive. He made it a rule to use them all. Indeed, Lord & Thomas personnel were, in theory at least, supposed to use their clients' products—smoke Lucky Strikes, use Pepsodent, listen to R.C.A., travel on the New York Central Railroad and never the Pennsylvania, drink Schenley whiskey, watch R.K.O. films, use Goodyear tires, wear Chanel perfume, and eat Quaker Oats for breakfast! One morning, Lasker passed one of his employees smoking a Chesterfield. He looked daggers at him and said in a frosty tone, but with a glint of humor in his eyes: "Mr. Smith, I presume your wife has a private income." Of course, Albert Lasker never organized a single board meeting. As the owner of 95% of shares in the agency, it was he alone who decided on policy. Lasker was by this time the richest man in the history of advertising and had made his fortune solely through advertising. Yet he was driven not by the desire to make money, but by curiosity. When he was nearly fifty, Lasker bought a property a few miles west of Lakeforest, the most fashionable neighborhood in Chicago. Compared with his new home, his house in Glencoe was like a postage stamp next to a Rubens. Millroad Farm, known to the Lasker family as "The Farm," covered around 570 acres and consisted of twenty-seven buildings. In all, it cost $3.5 million, which was a lot of money for a property in 1920, when dollars were still dollars and business-men were kings. Lasker's property was probably the most impressive in the whole of America, from coast to coast. The main house consisted of fifty rooms. It was surrounded by greenery. Around 300 acres had been landscaped and nearly 120 acres consisted of real gardens, although Lasker was incapable of telling the differ-ence between a tulip and a begonia. Fortunately, he hired good gardeners. The end result featured miles of pruned hedges, trees planted symmetrically in perfect har-mony with the landscape, and a swimming pool thirty-five yards long by fifteen yards wide. There was a garage for twelve cars and a projection room that was Lasker's pride and joy. Movies could be screened for fifty people, who sat in wide, deep armchairs. Lasker maintained that he had this private movie theater built so that nobody could complain if, in the middle of a movie, he insulted the bad guy or encouraged the hero out loud. Each of the property's buildings was air condi-tioned, something that was rare at the time. One of the most unusual features of all, however, was the eighteen-hole golf course, one of the only

private golf courses

in America at the time. It had cost $1 million and Bobby Jones, the famous cham-pion, regarded it as one of the best courses in America. Fifty employees looked after the property. Some of them slept in special dormitories, while others came from a neighboring village in buses provided by Lasker, who was the largest employer in Lakeforest. Whenever Lasker hired a new butler, he would warn him to be prepared for the fact that he might invite anywhere from ten to two hundred guests for dinner and that he might give him only one hour's warning. At this time,

Lasker was particularly close friends with John Hertz, the creator of the Yellow Cab

"Light a Lucky and you'll never

taxi company and the rental car company which bears his name. They were con-

miss sweets that make you fat."

tinually at each other's homes and, as Hertz put it, they lived together for twenty

What nerve! A cigarette present-

years. Hertz was a very different kind of person from Lasker. Born in

ed as a substitute for candy,

Czechoslovakia, he had worked as a journalist in Chicago. He founded the Yellow

which makes you fat and which

Cab Company in 1915. The taxi business in Chicago at the time was full of gang-

you eat mechanically all day long!

sters, and pretty dangerous ones at that. Hertz bought a house in Miami Beach,

which was just beginning to be developed in the 1920s, and persuaded Lasker to

join him. Lasker bought a plot 330 yards wide, overlooking the sea at 49/25 Collins

Avenue, right next door to Hertz, and construction work began. From this time on,

he spent most of his winter vacations in Florida. Lasker and Hertz became known

as the "twins of Miami." Lasker seems to have been more conscious than ever of

his Jewishness, due in large part to the strongly anti-Semitic atmosphere in

Chicago. Given that he was Jewish and at odds with this environment, it was par-

ticularly satisfying for him to be rich. As a wealthy man, he could buy status.

asker never attended a religious service, but he regularly sent a generous

donation to one of the main synagogues in Chicago, and he was also a

friend of the rabbi. The latter came to see him one day and explained

that, instead of his generous donations, he would prefer it if Lasker

attended services and became a member of the congregation. Lasker

refused. The rabbi insisted, saying that if he attended services it would undoubted-

ly add to the prestige of the synagogue and make it easier for him, the rabbi, to do

his job. Lasker again declined and the rabbi asked him why. He replied that he did

not want an intermediary between God and himself. His daughter Mary once asked

him what her religion was. He replied that her religion was to be able to say at the

end of each day, as if God was listening to her, that she hadn't done anything wrong

that day, nothing that she should be ashamed about. After a few years, sales of

"Light a Lucky and you'll never miss sweets that make you fat"

Constance Talmadge

Constance Talmadge,
Charming Motion
Picture Star

INSTEAD of eating between meals ... instead of fattening sweets ... beautiful women keep youthful slenderness these days by smoking <u>Luckies</u>. The smartest and loveliest women of the modern stage take this means of keeping slender ... when others nibble fattening sweets, they light a <u>Lucky!</u>

<u>Lucky Strike</u> is a delightful blend of the world's finest tobaccos. These tobaccos are toasted—a costly extra process which develops and improves the flavor. That's why <u>Luckies</u> are a delightful alternative for fattening sweets. That's why there's real health in <u>Lucky Strike</u>. That's why folks say: "<u>It's good to smoke Luckies.</u>"

For years this has been no secret to those men who keep fit and trim. They know that <u>Luckies</u> steady their nerves and do not harm their physical condition. They know that <u>Lucky Strike</u> is the favorite cigarette of many prominent athletes, who must keep in good shape. They respect the opinions of 20,679 physicians who maintain that <u>Luckies</u> are less irritating to the throat than other cigarettes.

A reasonable proportion of sugar in the diet is recommended, but the authorities are overwhelming that too many fattening sweets are harmful and that too many such are eaten by the American people. So, for moderation's sake we say:—

"REACH FOR A <u>LUCKY</u> INSTEAD OF A SWEET."

Constance Talmadge,
Charming Motion
Picture Star

"It's toasted"

No Throat Irritation-No Cough.

LUCKY STRIKE "IT'S TOASTED" CIGARETTES

Reach for a Lucky instead of a sweet.

© 1929, The American Tobacco Co., Manufacturers

to coast radio hook-up every Saturday night through the National Broadcasting Company's network. The Lucky Strike Dance Orchestra in "The Tunes that made Broadway, Broadway."

Pepsodent began to drop. Lasker, a regular listener to M.O.C.N., a famous radio show followed by everybody in the country, concluded that Americans could be divided into three categories: people who used Pepsodent and were happy to use it; those who had tried it and wouldn't use it again; and those who would probably never try it. Out of a sense of honor, he decided to make a supreme effort to convince the last two categories. Edward Lasker, his son, was working at the time for the radio department of Lord & Thomas in New York and suggested an idea to him. There was a comedian who had been a flop in several shows but who was so talented that he would be a success if he were given good scripts. So Lasker ordered that he be tried for Pepsodent. The name of the actor was Bob Hope. Once again, history was made. At the same time, the

soap opera

was born. These were radio series designed to amuse and captivate women at home. The first, the story of Mary Marling, sponsored by Kleenex, was a great success. Lasker did not manage his office in a conventional way and never turned it into an institution like Young and Rubicam, for example. It was run in a very eccentric fashion. Lasker hated committees as much as he disliked graphics and charts. An administrator was for him someone who has no brain. He loved above all stimulation, ideas, and originality. Lord & Thomas was not an organization, but a series of more or less autonomous groups, with Lasker, the dictator, at the top. He had a very unusual technique for winning arguments. He would become strangely calm, almost docile. "If you bang on the table, the other guy will do the same," he explained, "and it becomes difficult to win." Lasker always got to the office early in the morning. He was very punctual and expected the same of other people. His office in the Palmolive Building was separated from the rest of the agency by a small hall and a reception room. To go in and out, you had to go through doorways.

Lasker passed through them as if he were in a trance. On arrival, he spent an hour carefully reading his mail, scribbling a note in pencil on most of the letters and redirecting the correspondence to the person he felt was best placed to deal with the problem. When he was dictating, the little barks and hesitations of his speech disappeared. Then he would go to the barber shop next door to his office. He sometimes received clients there while he was being shaved, like an eighteenth-century monarch. One of his secretaries remembered that he was incapable of doing anything slowly. He liked to hire young people so that they could be trained. One of his advertisements for the agency, in the middle of the 1930s, had the heading: "Trees die from the top, and so do advertising agencies." Lasker paid high salaries to people he regarded as important, and low salaries to everyone else. He could be extremely generous, but at the same time very stingy. He rewarded the man who had introduced him to Mahler by doubling his salary. But a modest employee had

Lasker had the Lucky packaging redesigned by the famous designer Raymond Loewy. His campaign featuring actresses and opera singers had every woman smoking!

LUCKY STRIKE MEANS FINE TOBACCO!
"Old Belt"...Virginia tobacco painted from life by John Steuart Curry

So Round, So Firm, So Fully Packed — So Free and Easy On The Draw

a lot of trouble getting his weekly salary raised from $35 to $40. Even before he had become a big success, one copywriter came to him with two lines of text that pleased Lasker so much that he gave him a $10,000 bonus on the spot.

In truth, aside from the top posts in the agency, he did not need to pay high salaries. Young people starting out in advertising all wanted to be trained at Lord & Thomas and were ready to work for a modest salary. But the number of salaries paid by his agency nevertheless always scared Lasker. On one occasion, returning from a vacation in the South, he called for a general meeting of the Chicago agency. Nearly two hundred men and women gathered in the hall. Lasker, livid, shouted: "What! I pay salaries to all these people?" In 1931, in the middle of the Great Depression, he cut salaries by 25% and 30%. On February 13, 1933, he fired more than fifty men and women who had been at the agency for years. All this he did while continuing to pay himself a salary of $3 million a year. As the sole owner of the agency, of course, he could do exactly what he wanted. Lasker was one of those fortunate men who become more handsome as they grow older. As a young man, nobody would have said he was good looking, but in his sixties and seventies he became like

a prophet

from the Scriptures. His biggest assets were his large eyes, which were a deep, dark, sparkling brown in color and had a liquid brilliance. But Lasker was not very interested in beautiful features. One day, Cone, one of his chief colleagues at the time, was defending someone Lasker did not like: "At least admit that he has a handsome face, Mr. Lasker!" The reply came back: "Mr. Cone, you and I have strong faces." Lasker hated dogs, cats, airplanes, trains that were late, being bored, things that were done badly or shoddily, women who thought a lot of themselves, and, above all, being wrong. He entered psychoanalysis and the diagnosis was unequivocal:

Lasker had a strong guilt complex. The psychoanalysis was intended to help him lose it. His psychoanalyst once told him that he loved Dali's paintings showing Italian cities, so Lasker promptly offered him two Dali paintings of this kind. Working with Lasker was particularly traumatic, especially when he was tense. He was always on everybody's back. Incapable of leaving his colleagues alone, he harassed them endlessly: "Have you tried that? Why haven't you done this?" He was quite capable of asking for a new campaign on December 22, demanding that it be ready for December 26, completely forgetting about Christmas, and then, worse still, forgetting that he had ever asked for the campaign in the first place. Many people at Lord & Thomas worked Sundays and sometimes all through the night. "Think while you are shaving," he said one day to Benton. One of Lasker's practices was to never tell people what he thought of them. Of course, the turnover of staff at Lord & Thomas was considerable. People left to earn more money elsewhere or because they couldn't handle the pressure any more. Lasker the virtuoso could create good professionals, but he couldn't keep them. He would use up all the air around him, leaving none for the others. He trained people, then lost them or let them leave. His behavior with advertisers was just as extraordinary. Nobody in the history of advertising, not even Stanley Resor or J. Walter Thomson, whom Lasker admired, ever dared to treat their clients the way he did. He was in the habit of saying: "This would be a great profession if it wasn't for the clients!" He was quite capable of ringing a big shot at General Motors to ask him to come straight away because he didn't like the way things were going at Frigidaire. He was never in the least frightened of his clients, although he would have been upset to lose a client like Lucky Strike. When you were a friend of Lasker's, you were perfect, of course. But if men or women didn't live up to his expectations, he would become intensely disillusioned with them. He liked people too much, and wanted at all costs to do them good. And when his affection dwindled, he was left naked. But even then, he maintained an extraordinary generosity of spirit. For his friends, he would have gone without anything. On one occasion, when sales of Pepsodent were falling, Lasker told the president of the company, Ken Smith, that he should be more aggressive. Smith replied that Pepsodent wasn't in such a bad position and that results weren't that bad. Lasker replied: "You remind me of the story of the guy who falls out of a window on the thirtieth floor and who says, as he's passing the fifteenth, 'So far so good!'" Suddenly, in July 1938, Lasker resigned as president of Lord & Thomas, although he retained ownership of the agency. Don Francisco replaced him, but it was a premature farewell and his retirement did not last long. In fact, Lasker was having a new nervous breakdown. He spent the autumn in California. His friends showered him with affection and attention, but he felt alone and depressed. One of his best friends, movie tycoon Louis Hayes, felt that he had to do something to help him. The best he could do was to find a woman he could marry, who might reawaken his interest in life. Hayes organized a series of invitations to dinners and soirées, and everyone passed the word to invite the prettiest unmarried women in the hope that Lasker would become interested in one of them. And that is exactly what happened. Her name was Doris Kenyon. She was an actress,

she was beautiful...

and she was already a widow. Lasker, impetuous and irresistible as usual, set about seducing her. He even managed to convince himself that he was in love with her, and she with him. They got married at the Waldorf Astoria on October 28, 1938, and left on the *Ile de France* for a honeymoon in Europe. But the marriage did not last long. Doris had never met a man so sensitive to the mildest of upsets. She found it exhausting. For his part, Lasker had never lived with a star. Usually he was the star, and he found it difficult to accept that his wife received more attention than he did. He decided to put an end to this difficult situation, and the details of the divorce were worked out. He emerged from this union more hurt than ever. On June 8, 1939, the divorce was pronounced in Reno. Lasker offered Doris a sum of money that was very generous in view of the brevity of their marriage. Doris, very dignified, refused. A few years later she married Arthur Rubinstein's brother-in-law.

I n 1939, Lasker was alone and depressed, but not resigned. He said to a friend: "I will find the wife who suits me, even if I have to marry ten." Soon after, he met Mary Reinhart, who had been married to Paul Reinhart while she was working at the Reinhart Gallery. Indeed, she was the first art dealer to have a diploma in art history. After her divorce, she had had to earn her living. The art market was regarded as a risky market, especially during the Depression, so she started making dress patterns in collaboration with *Vogue* magazine. *Vogue* made the patterns and Mary sold them to stores and branches for 15¢ each. Because of the Depression, more and more women were obliged to make their own dresses. After a fairly slow start, business started to prosper for Mary. When she met Albert Lasker, she was comfortably off. Lasker always admired her professional success. At the time, Mary lived with her mother in a penthouse with a terrace decorated with flowers. She owned a De Chirico, which hung above the fireplace. Following his second marriage, Lasker decided to give up his extraordinary property at Millroad Farm. His lawyer advised him that he would not be able to get its full value and suggested that he donate it to an institution. Within an hour, Lasker had made a phone call in which he offered Millroad, which was worth nearly $4 million, to the University of Chicago. Thus he abandoned the luxurious property where he had lived for thirteen years and thereby cut himself off from the past, persuading himself that such a visible and grandiose property was now an anachronism. Very quickly, the University of Chicago realized that it would not be able to maintain such a property. After attempting to use it as a horticultural research center, then as a center for seminars, the whole property, including the golf course, was split up and divided into lots to make houses. The manor house was sold for the paltry sum of $110,000. On June 24, 1940, Albert and Mary married in New York. Their honeymoon began with a cruise around Long Island. They then went to Philadelphia for the Republican Convention. Once the Convention was over, their honeymoon continued on Lake Michigan aboard a yacht. At night, movies were screened on deck. They visited Ernst Mahler. Lasker seemed happier than ever. In 1941, the couple settled in New York for good, renting a six-story house at 26 Beekman Place with a view of the East River. In the spring of 1942, Lasker resigned from the board of directors of the University of Chicago. This was the seed for another decision that he seemed to have taken abruptly at the end of the same year. At the end of a lunch, he went home instead of going to the office and announced to Mary that he would never go back to the agency. It was the end of forty-four years of Lasker rule. He never returned to the office, abandoning the agency that still brought him more than $1 million net a year. There were several reasons for his choice. He was tired of advertising and felt that the business was becoming increasingly mechanical. The new generation of executives who now dealt with the clients seemed to him, in truth, not to be up to the job. Also, he wanted to devote himself to public service. Above all, however, his son Edward had decided he would not take over the reins. The problem arose of how to bring Lord & Thomas to an end. There were several possibilities. Merger with another agency was one, but that would take time and require negotiations. Selling it was another, but Lasker decided that the name Lord & Thomas would disappear with him and it would be difficult to sell an agency whose company name was so much of its worth. He could make a gift of the agency, but that would create very complex problems. In fact, although Lasker did not want to see the name of Lord & Thomas survive after his departure, he was

Lasker was bold enough to tackle a subject that was totally taboo in the America of the 1920s, through ads that were direct and a form of sale that spared women any embarrassment.

determined that his colleagues should not be abandoned and that clients, some of whom had been with the agency for fifty years, should not be thrown into the street like tramps. The right solution, even though it would be complicated to achieve, would involve liquidating Lord & Thomas while creating a new company that would take on his colleagues and clients. At this time, the three most important directors of the company were Emerson Foote in New York, Fairfax Cone in Chicago, and Tom Belding in Los Angeles. These three men had all been recommended as successors to Albert Lasker. Lasker hardly knew Belding, liked and admired Foote, and had always been close to Cone. Lasker had Cone come to New York on December 16, 1942, and organized a meeting with him and Foote. The discussions lasted three weeks almost without interruption. In the beginning, the idea was to create not one but three companies: one in New York, one in Chicago, and one on the West Coast. But it quickly became clear that it would be simpler to create a single company by dividing the capital equally between the three directors, with each one retaining his own territory but working in constant cooperation with the others. Just before Christmas of the same year, the Laskers went to Chicago and the last details were finalized. Lord & Thomas was dissolved, and at the same time the agency Foote, Cone and Bedding, still known today by the initials was created. It only cost the new owners $150,000. Three young men, who didn't have a cent, who had never worked in the same room together, found themselves with clients who had already invested $750 million in advertising. Lasker informed all his clients himself, asking them to carry on with the new agency, even though he was no longer part of it. On December 30, a team of workers took down the Lord & Thomas sign from the Palmolive Building. And Lasker was able to say to himself, "If it collapses, people will say that it could not work without me. If it works, they will say that I trained my people so well that it couldn't fail." Lasker's final piece of advice was "Watch the electricity bills," an appropriate farewell remark for someone who had two hang-ups: electricity and telephone bills. This man, who could spend $50,000 on a single object without qualms, became hysterical if he thought the electricity bill was too high. He always had an aversion to the telephone and long distance calls in particular. Whenever he called his lawyer in Chicago from New York, once the business problems were out of the way, he would give him a number of messages for his friends in Chicago so that he wouldn't have to call them himself. Similarly, electricity was an obsession for him. If he was in the agency after everyone had gone home, he would go round all the offices and turn off the lights one by one. Whenever he visited his friends the Blocks in Chicago, he would comment on the fact that their paintings were permanently illuminated by spotlights, even during the day. He would ritually exclaim: "Good heavens, can't you see well enough during the day!" Despite his retirement, Lasker remained passionately interested in the Pepsodent venture. Although he no longer had any income from it as an advertiser, he remained one of the biggest shareholders. He hoped that his wife and children would benefit from this, the biggest investment that he had made in his life, after his death. But suddenly, in June 1944,

Initially called Celluwipes when it was created in 1954, this product was soon renamed Kleenex' Kerchiefs. This was in turn shortened to Kleenex and promoted by Lasker, subsequently becoming the generic name for all paper handkerchiefs.

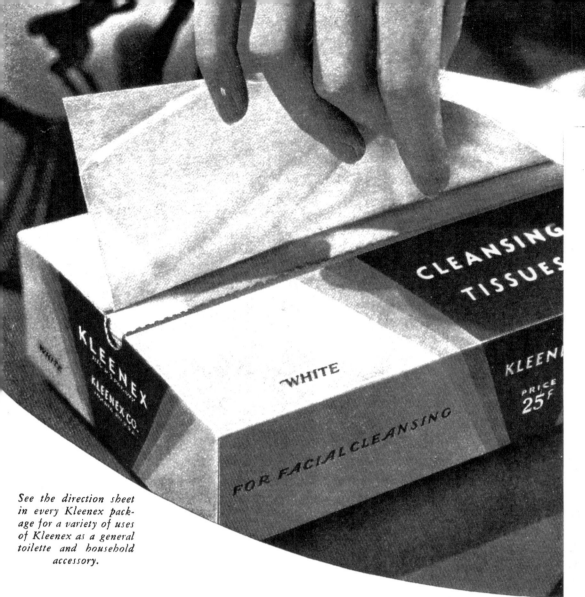

KLEENEX · WHITE · FOR FACIAL CLEANSING · CLEANSING TISSUES · PRICE 25¢

See the direction sheet in every Kleenex package for a variety of uses of Kleenex as a general toilette and household accessory.

OFFICE WORKERS *find Kleenex invaluable for handkerchiefs, for applying make-up, for towels, and for removing creams after the daytime cleansing treatment.*

MOTHERS *have discovered that Kleenex makes perfect handkerchiefs for children. It costs less than laundering.*

Now ... try Kleenex for Handkerchiefs

It is softer, more hygienic, and costs less than laundering handkerchiefs ... ideal for colds and hay fever ... coupon brings free sample.

YOU know what Kleenex Tissues are ... those soft, dainty tissues that smart women are using to remove cold cream.

But did you also know that Kleenex is rapidly replacing handkerchiefs among progressive people? Doctors are recommending it. Nose and throat specialists are using Kleenex in their office work.

Kleenex is so much more sanitary. You use it just once, then discard it forever. Cold germs are discarded too, instead of being carried about in an insanitary handkerchief, to reinfect the user and infect others.

And Kleenex is infinitely more comfortable. You know how irritating a damp handkerchief becomes. But with Kleenex, every tissue that touches your face is soft, dry, gentle and absorbent. And soothing.

Kleenex is a great saving, as the cost is way below that of laundering a handkerchief.

A Kleenex Tissue is the size of a handkerchief. It's very soft. Each tissue comes from the box immaculately clean and fresh.

You can buy Kleenex in a large or small size package. And in three tints, besides white. All of these colors are guaranteed absolutely pure and safe. Buy Kleenex at any drug, dry goods or department store.

Let us send you a sample of Kleenex, just to prove to you how lovely Kleenex is. The coupon below will bring you a generous sample absolutely free.
Kleenex Company, Chicago, Ill.

FOR COLDS AND HAY FEVER — *Other people appreciate your use of Kleenex during colds instead of the germ-filled handkerchief which is a menace to those about you.*

FREE TRIAL PACKAGE

Kleenex Company, Lake-Michigan Bldg., Chicago, Ill. Please send me a trial supply of Kleenex free of charge.

Name..

Street..

City..State................

Lever Brothers bought Pepsodent for $10 million cash and Lasker, a minority shareholder, had to sell his shares. When George Washington Hill of American Tobacco Co. died in 1946, the last remaining links recalling his career were broken. Lasker was now completely free of his past. From this time on, he devoted himself to his new friends, including Anna Rosenbert, and to trips to Paris and Israel. His energy and his money were concentrated on two centers of interest: medical research and painting. The

lasker foundation,

still active today, did important work in birth control, while the American Cancer Society was developed to fight against cancer and carry out research into treatments for cardiovascular and arteriosclerotic diseases. Given his antipathy toward

Sensitive, perceptive, and passionate, this tall, thin man possessed unusual physical energy. He had a great sense of humor and everyone enjoyed his company.

art directors and layout artists, the second activity was more surprising: he fell in love with painting, to such a degree that during the last years of his life he put together one of the most impressive collections in the history of art. He never bought anything he didn't like, and when people told him he was wrong, he said, "Let me make my own mistakes, it's the only way to learn." In fact, he seems to have learned quickly, because when he died he left two Renoirs, nine of Matisse's finest works, including *Pineapple and Anemones*, a Corot, a Cézanne, four Braques, a Monet, seventeen Picassos, two Rouaults, a Miró, seventy-eight various gouaches, ten Dufys, twenty-four Salvador Dalis, two Van Goghs, two Chagalls, three Latours, four Utrillos, three Redons, one Degas, one Modigliani, one Manet (*Julia*), one Soutine, one Foujita and Toulouse-Lautrec's *Woman in Red*. He loved painting so much that he even, one day, went so far as to buy half a dozen of Marie Laurencin's paintings to give as Christmas presents. He celebrated his seventieth birthday in Paris on May 1, 1950, in the company of Danny Kaye. Two years later, on May 30, 1952, he died in New York at the age of seventy-three, the biggest tycoon in the history of advertising. He left behind $11 million. He had earned $1 billion. What has happened to the agency he left behind? Two of those he chose to carry on his creative work, Emerson Foote and Tom Belding, retired in 1954. Fairfax Cone retired in 1970. But the agency was still strong and ready for the changes brought about by globalization. Norman Brown, who was in charge of the group until 1991, formed an alliance with Publicis, the agency founded by Marcel Bleustein-Blanchet. Then his successor, Bruce Mason, brought BCB into the holding True North. And in 1998, after protracted wrangling between the French and the American agency, True North and Publicis parted company, enemy brothers. Just one year later, the F.C.B. and Bozell networks merged. What would Lasker, the acrobat, the Mister 100,000 volts of advertising, have thought? Nobody knows. What remains today is a high-powered group which is made up of 172 agencies and is present in 82 countries, a network that achieves business of $8.3 billion, recognized for its expertise in all areas of marketing and communications. The leading group in the United States and the sixth in the world, F.C.B. continues on its way in a harsh competitive environment. But then hadn't Lasker thought of everything?

burnett

ate: October 1959; place: office 14A, the New Prudential Building, Chicago. If you were to look through the glazed opening in the projection room, you would be able to make out a curious collection of people. The seats, which seem to have been placed in a predetermined arrangement, as well as the age and the behavior of the people occupying them, suggest that none of this has happened by chance and that you are seeing a sort of royal court, or at times even a court of law. Sitting close together around the sides of the room, against the walls, are at least twelve pale, tense young people. In the center of the room, around a large table of dark wood, with more space between them, sit a few older men. Their faces are more tanned, but they are scarcely less tense. Their names are Norman Muse, Burt Manning, Charlie Blackmore, and Draper Daniels. To the right of Draper Daniels, presiding, is a strange man who looks to be well into his sixties.

You can see instantly that he is the king of this assembly. He is half bald, with a sharply protruding forehead, not dissimilar to that of Henry Kissinger. His face is almost smooth, or at least remarkably free from wrinkles for a man of his age. You can see, even though he is seated, that he is a short man. His drooping shoulders accentuate his strikingly pear-shaped body. His slightly bulging eyes and his pronounced double chin irresistibly call to mind some kind of toad, an image reinforced by the croaking sound of his voice. The outsize lower lip, like the rim of a chamber pot, gives this person, who is a godsend for caricaturists, yet another distinctive feature. The lapels of his dark and creased suit are covered in ash from the Marlboro ciga-

Leo Burnett was born October 21, 1891, in St. Johns, Michigan. The son of a grocer who was keen on advertising, he went on to single-handly create the School of Chicago, which was the envy of Madison Avenue, the Mecca of advertising. People even talked of the "Burnettization" of American advertising.

rettes that he chain-smokes. This man's name is Leo Burnett. On this fine late summer day in 1959, his advertising agency was celebrating twenty-four years of business. It was ranked fourth in the world, with business of $120 million. In New York, a city which prided itself on being the Mecca of advertising, everybody was talking of the

burnettization

of American advertising and could not get over the fact that New York was being trumped by Chicago in the person of this strange man. But we should begin at the beginning, which can be traced back to October 21, 1891, in St. Johns, Michigan. Leo Burnett, the future celebrity, was supposed to have been called George. It is thought that the registrar, due to a sudden whim, or out of distraction or malice, saddled him with the name of Leo. One thing is certain, this was not the name his parents had chosen for him. His father was a grocer and did his own advertising. Every evening after dinner, Mr. Burnett senior, equipped with a large black pencil and a sheet of wrapping paper, created an advertisement for his store, delivered it to the local newspaper the following day and waited for customers. While still in primary school, young Leo began working for a printer. Later, he worked for a year as a teacher in a rural school so that he could save enough money to enroll at the University of Michigan. Once he entered college, he continued to earn his living as a writer of birthday cards for Mark's, the largest store in Ann Arbor. Leo graduated in 1914. The following fall, by chance he met a relative who told him that there was a vacancy for a reporter on the *Peoria (Ill.) Journal* for the extraordinary salary of $18 a week. By the following Monday, the *Peoria (Ill.) Journal* had a new reporter among its ranks. Not content with his $18 a week, Leo sold articles to magazines, as well as a few stories. During this time, he had stayed in contact with a friend from college who had settled in Detroit. This friend was convinced, with some jus tification, that the automobile industry was certain to grow, and he had begun working as the editor of Packard's in-house magazine. In this capacity, he received the sumptuous salary of $40 a week and a membership card for the Detroit Athletic Club. This was enough to leave Leo Burnett drooling with envy. A short while after, Fred Scott, Leo's English professor in college, informed him that the Cadillac Motor Company was looking for an editor for their in-house magazine. Leo was hired, and it was through this post that he would later enter the company's

advertising department. It is worth noting that, of all the great pioneers of advertising, he was the only one who began his career with an advertiser. In Cadillac's advertising service, he met the person who was to have the biggest impact on him, prompting him to embark on a career in advertising. This man was Theodore MacManus, one of the most famous copywriters of the period. From this time on, advertising became much more than a just a job for Burnett; it became a religion.

One of the first mythical creatures to spring from the mind of Burnett, the Green Giant character is known to people around the world.

ollowing the outbreak of World War I, Leo Burnett was drafted. He came out a private, without ever having left Lake Michigan. When he returned to Cadillac, the company was in turmoil. A large number of executives left to form LaFayette Motors in Indianapolis, and Leo joined them as advertising manager. Unfortunately, 1921 was a particularly difficult year for luxury products, and LaFayette struggled. Leo Burnett got a job with Homer McKee, the city's leading advertising agency, where he quickly established himself as a copywriter, receiving a salary of $15,000 a year. Burnett

had at last found his true vocation. A friend of his in Indianapolis recalled that one Saturday evening he took his wife to the movies. When he came out of the movie theater, his wife pointed out a small lit window in an enormous dark façade. "Oh, that's Leo Burnett's office," replied her husband, "He's always there." This was in 1930; Leo Burnett was thirty-nine. Unlike Lasker or Rubicam, he did not appear to be interested in a personal career. There was no sign that he was consumed by ambition. He simply seemed to have a passion for advertising, with no regard for honors, prizes, or even money. It was at this time that Erwin Wasey's famous agency contacted Burnett and invited him to manage the setting up of their new office in

chicago.

This was a real challenge. At the time, the best talents were all being snapped up by the New York agencies, and Burnett, in charge of the creative side of things, was faced with a real shortage of creative talent. He thus brought a copywriter with him from Indianapolis, De Witt O'Kieffe, an avid reader of Homer and Virgil, and he completed the team with Winters, Art Kudner, and Sherman Ellis. Everything went well until 1935, when Kudner broke away to create his own agency, taking the Buick, Goodyear, and General Motors accounts with him. The situation deteriorated for Erwin Wasey. No personal projects germinated in Leo Burnett's head. His sole preoccupation was to create good advertising, which he did, tirelessly. In the end, the clients themselves persuaded Burnett to open his own agency. O'Kieffe also put pressure on him, saying that if he didn't, he would go and work in New York. Burnett thus took the plunge, mortgaging his house and borrowing against his life insurance policy. He was almost forty-four and had three clients: Minnesota Valley, which would be better known later as the Green Giant brand, the textile company Realsilk Hosiery, and Hoover. There were eight employees for billings of

$1 million. This wasn't really the best moment to be starting up an advertising agency. It was the middle of the Depression. Some 280,000 families were destitute. Salaries were low. Women were being encouraged to go out to work so that homes would have two incomes. From the beginning of the Depression, in 1929, consumers were hunting for cheap goods, a phenomenon that led, at the beginning of the 1930s, to the big revolution in distribution with the appearance of self-service supermarkets. Sirloin steak cost 30¢ a pound, a bottle of Heinz Ketchup 10¢, and Marlboro cigarettes 10¢ a packet. The Chicagoland chain, an ancestor of McDonald's, offered a coffee and a donut for 10¢ and for 15¢ added a fried egg, three pieces of bacon, and buttered toast.

United Airlines advertised its East Coast-West Coast flights by offering a free return flight to all wives accompanying their husbands. General Motors had just manufactured its one millionth car. The new Oldsmobile was on sale for $675 with credit at 6%, and gasoline cost less than 22¢ a gallon. The

leo burnett inc.

was inaugurated on Monday, August 5, 1935, at 360 Michigan Avenue. This date coincided exactly with the founding of the city of Chicago two hundred years earlier. That Monday, when Leo Burnett got up at 6:00 A.M., the temperature was already a sticky 77°F and it continued to rise throughout the day, reaching 86°F with 83% humidity. The team moved into five little offices and everyone got down

This early ad for Green Giant features an illustration in the style of Norman Rockwell, which creates a rural family atmosphere.

to work. By this time, Leo had already been married for seventeen years to Naomi Geddes. When he met her in 1917, she was working as a checkout girl in a restaurant near the Cadillac Motor Company. In fact, she was a student and she shared his strong interest in literature. Later, she described their first twenty years together as a conventional suburban marriage, without major incident–apart from the opening of the little advertising agency on Michigan Avenue in 1935. From the day it opened, Leo Burnett's agency had two distinguishing features, which eventually became legendary. The first was the presence, at reception, of a large bowl full of red apples, which were replaced each day. One malicious journalist wrote: "It won't be long before Leo Burnett will be selling apples on the street, instead of giving them away." The second feature was the company logo: a hand reaching for the stars. This symbol was derived from one of Leo Burnett's sayings, which he had made a rule of work: "If you reach for the stars, you may not quite get one, but you won't come up with a handful of mud either." Determined to show Madison Avenue what a good team in Chicago was capable of, Burnett went to war, armed with his own convictions. Firstly, he wanted people to say "What a great product!" and not "What a great advertisement!" Secondly, he believed that strong ideas did not necessarily need to be expressed in words. Thirdly, he believed that "lurking in every product that deserves success is a reason for being and a reason for buying which is deeply felt by the manufacturer and which, if captured and communicated, is the best of all possible advertising, because it is honest and believable. The trick is to make it interesting and exciting." Leo was not content with simply enunciating principles such as these, he worked to put them into practice. He delegated all administrative tasks to other people and concentrated on developing strategies and concepts. He supervised the process of putting ideas into practice and the implementation of campaigns.

This ad alluding to the origins of the Leo Burnett Company features the famous apples which became an integral part of the company's identity.

FOUNDED
AUGUST 5, 1935

Only a bunch of optimists would have opened
an ad agency on a day like that—and we still are

"god is in the details!"

he exclaimed one day, "No detail is unimportant." So Burnett demanded perfection in form, texture, and color. He worked hard to achieve this and was very demanding of his colleagues. Up every day at 5:00 A.M., he worked for two hours at his home in Glencoe before having breakfast and getting the train to Chicago. He would emerge from the station lost in thought, and was sometimes known to jump in a taxi and shout "Fourteenth floor please!" Leo arrived at the office before 8:30 A.M. and went through the desks of the copywriters and art directors. He was still at the office late in the evening, chewing large black pencils in the company of the agency's other creative minds. He often returned home by taxi around midnight, and sometimes continued working. As William Tyler observed, "It must be disconcerting for three highly intelligent children to see their father only if they happen to get up for a glass of water during the night."

a nd yet, despite Burnett's best efforts, the agency's first year was difficult. A bad harvest led the main client, the Minnesota Valley Canning Company, to slash its budget. Billings for the financial year were $600,000, which was $300,000 less than forecast. The year 1937 was an important one, not so much in terms of growth, but in terms of recruitment. Burnett hired Richard Heath, entrusting him with the job of finding

How Green "Umbrellas" make better Campbell Tomatoes

Another famous brand is born: Campbell, the famous brand of soup whose red and white cans made a certain Andy Warhol famous.

64

new clients, a task he had previously dealt with himself. Thanks to the combination of Heath's commercial know-how and Burnett's talent for advertising, the agency rapidly began to expand. Together, the men were able to achieve what one person alone had been incapable of. As Draper Daniels, one of the first employees, put it: "It's Leo who writes the good word, but it's Dick Heath who spreads it." In short, you could say that Heath was prophet to Burnett's messiah! The results were immediate. In 1938, six new clients joined the agency, including Pure Oil, which later became Union Oil, and the Brown Shoe Company, which would still be working with Burnett thirty-five years later. In 1939, Leo Burnett Co. occupied the whole of the fifteenth story of the building and won its first million-dollar account. This was a collective account for the American Institute of Butcher's Meat. Not only did they have to compete with twenty-eight other advertising agencies, but in addition they had to present the campaign in fifty different cities. It took ten weeks. In 1942, the agency entered the competition for the

santa fe railroad

account, but only had four days to prepare their presentation. O'Kieffe, the agency's best copywriter, jumped aboard the "Super Chief" and made the trip to California while writing his impressions of the train during the journey. When he arrived in California, he telegraphed his notes to Chicago and Leo used them to put together a great presentation, which was very original for the period. It was the first time a campaign had been based on the concept of the "travel notebook." The agency won the account despite the competition of forty other agencies, and kept it for twenty-three years. In the same year, Leo bought a 200-acre farm near Lake Zurich in Illinois. That changed his wife Naomi's life, but not Leo's. He simply abandoned golf so that he could look after the gardening and the planting. At the wheel of a small truck, he traveled around his property supervising the planting of some 20,000 trees and shrubs. On the one hundred acres behind the farm, there were two marshes. Leo

The competition for the Santa

had the idea of transforming one of them into a ten-acre lake. Alarmed by this proj-

Fe account was won with days

ect, his wife suggested selling the farm and buying another which already had a lake,

to spare thanks to the idea of

but Leo wanted to create his own. He proceeded to do just that, with the aid of enor-

getting a copywriter to make

mous earthmovers and by means of drilling. His only fear was that he might find oil

the trip and send his impres-

when all he was looking for was water. In 1947, Leo Burnett's business hit $10 mil-

sions back to the agency.

lion. The trade magazine *Advertising Age* rated the agency twenty-sixth in the world.

In 1949, the agency acquired Pillsbury (flour), Kellogg's, Campbell Soup, and the

Tea Council, as well as a large account for Procter & Gamble devoted to researching

new products. This was also the year of the first sponsored television shows, pro-

duced by Burnett for Hoover. The year 1950 proved to be a significant one for the

agency, which passed the threshold of $22 million in billings, overtaking the Foote,

Cone and Belding agency (run by Lasker's successors) to become the biggest agency

in Chicago. The Minnesota Valley Canning Company eventually came round to

Leo's way of thinking, and changed its name to the Green Giant Company.

f course, 1954 was also particularly important for the agency, which by this time had more than 540 employees and had climbed to eighth place, with business of more than $50 mil-

lion. Above all, however, 1954 saw the birth of a legend in

advertising: Marlboro. Representatives of the Philip Morris Company were visit-

ing all the agencies to see which one they would entrust with their Marlboro filter

cigarette. Leo met them at the entrance to his office and invited them in. The floor

was littered with layouts, which Burnett commented on. The people from Philip

Morris must have been pleased, because they immediately awarded the account to

the agency. But they still had to work out the details. At the time, filter cigarettes

were regarded as effeminate, so the problem was how to make

Santa Fe
.. to the colorful Southwest

That's right, chico.
And "all the way" in the finest modern style —
and now on new and faster schedules.
For Santa Fe feels a great debt to nature for the colorful,
romantic land through which it runs — and
a real responsibility to you, to take you through it
in the finest way.

SANTA FE SYSTEM LINES
Serving the West and Southwest

a masculine brand, a cigarette that men could smoke in public without risking ridicule. Burnett began by changing the packaging, replacing the beige-white color by a deep red with a V shape formed by white space. As for the visual to be used in the advertisements, there was only one question: what was the most masculine type of man? Through research and meetings, agreement was reached on the cowboy. The first Marlboro advertisement appeared in January 1955, showing a virile cowboy and his cigarettes. From that day on, the filter cigarette market would never be the same.

Later, under pressure from Philip Morris, who feared the public was growing weary, advertisements featured other virile figures wearing tattoos. But at Leo's instigation, they returned to cowboys, a decision which proved benefi-

A scene familiar to many, especially

cial to the brand and led to one of the

children. The Green Giant, a kindly,

greatest successes in the history of adver-

good-humored giant towering over

tising. In 1956, the Leo Burnett Co. had to

his land—a land of plenty, a prom-

find new premises, so it moved to the

ised land of tasty vegetables.

brand new Prudential Insurance

Company skyscraper in Chicago, occupying five whole stories, from the eleventh to the fifteenth. It was faced with the classic challenge faced by all large agencies: how could it retain its creativity? In the mid-1950s, marketing and research began to dominate advertising, but Burnett stuck to his belief that creativity was the key tool. By October 1959, the point where we started this chapter, the agency had annual billings of nearly $120 million and had started using its first computer, an IBM Ramac 305 Electronic Data designed for administrative tasks and accounting. A profit-sharing scheme for employees was worked out. Leo, now a rich man, bought made-to-measure suits, but he had a knack of always looking as though he had just stepped out of a suitcase. As one of his colleagues put it, "Every morning he arrived in a freshly crumpled suit."

eo worked as hard as ever and got home in the evening with his face covered in pencil marks. David Ogilvy claimed that he had refused a merger between his agency and that of Burnett because the latter was the only man he knew who worked harder than he did. The idea that Leo might call him at 2:00 A.M. to ask to see him in Chicago for breakfast with ideas for a new campaign was more than he could bear. However, there had been a slight change. After a mild heart attack in 1947, Leo had been obliged to watch his blood pressure. It was only twelve years later, in 1959, that he agreed to relax his schedule by staying home on Fridays. He immediately invented the

The year 1954 marked the beginning of another legend. Filter cigarettes at this time had an effeminate image. The packaging was changed in favor of red with a white V-shaped space and, the Marlboro cowboy was born.

"farm sessions," when an army of copywriters, graphic designers, advertising directors, and project managers would be summoned to his property on Friday evenings or Saturday mornings, resulting in an extra day for everyone else. When they left the office at the end of the week, everyone was careful to double lock their files in a drawer, because Leo would always be the first to arrive on Mondays and would look around to see what had been done in the agency during his absence. There were also long internal presentation meetings. These were verita-

New from Philip Morris
Marlboro
FILTER CIGARETTES
Marlboro
The new easy-drawing filter cigarette that delivers
the goods on flavor. Long size. Popular filter price.
Light up a Marlboro and be glad you've changed to a filte

ble boxing matches, which took place in the famous office 14A, where Leo presided, judged, praised, criticized, thundered, complimented, suggested, inspired, condemned, encouraged, and laid down the law. If he disliked a campaign, he looked dejected and his lower lip, which already stuck out, swelled up and hung down over his chin. His colleagues quickly learned to measure how well their work had been received according to what they called the Lip Protrusion Index. Indeed, they even graded the protrusion from one to ten, an LPI of five meaning extra nights of work, and an LPI of ten indicating you were on the verge of being fired. Everybody's work was discussed and dissected in front of everyone, but this cruel process was not inefficient, and the quality of the advertising produced by the agency hit new heights. Presentation meetings with clients were not lacking in suspense. No matter how hard they tried to keep the atmosphere calm, the heads of advertising could not prevent Leo Burnett from occasionally interrupting a meeting by shouting: "Hold everything, I have a much better idea!" The trade press all talked of the Chicago School, and the Chicago School was Leo Burnett. All the campaigns used by the growing number of branches bearing the Burnett name came out of Chicago. Since the beginning of the 1950s, Leo Burnett's agency had been actively involved in the meteoric growth of television. In 1949, there were less than a million viewers; in 1952, there were fifteen million viewers; in 1955, there were thirty million; and by the beginning of the 1960s, 87% of homes in America had television sets. By this time,

leo burnett & co.

had its own production company in Chicago, New York, Hollywood, and Toronto, using, among others, Mickey Rooney for Green Giant and Pillsbury, and Gary Moore for Hoover. The agency itself produced shows sponsored by its clients, but in 1965 CBS, NDL, and ABC came together to force the agencies to stop making

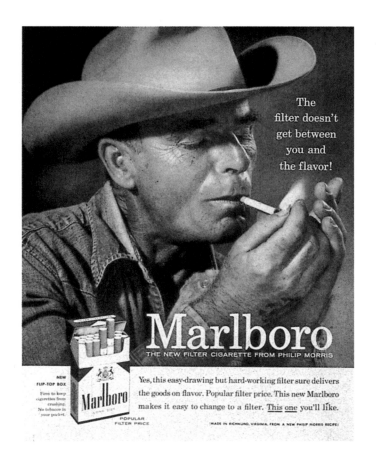

The
filter doesn't
get between
you and
the flavor!

Marlboro
THE NEW FILTER CIGARETTE FROM PHILIP MORRIS

NEW
FLIP-TOP BOX
Firm to keep
cigarettes from
crushing.
No tobacco in
your pocket.

Marlboro
LONG SIZE

POPULAR
FILTER PRICE

Yes, this easy-drawing but hard-working filter sure delivers
the goods on flavor. Popular filter price. This new Marlboro
makes it easy to change to a filter. This one you'll like.

MADE IN RICHMOND, VIRGINIA, FROM A NEW PHILIP MORRIS RECIPE!

shows, restricting them to commercials. At the end of 1965, the agency still had nearly all its original clients, in addition to Nestlé and United Airlines. It had 1,175 employees in Chicago alone. With billings of $174 million, it was the sixth most successful agency in the world. Leo's health had recently started to decline, although mentally he was as strong as ever. A form of diabetes caused him, from time to time, to pass out in dramatic fashion through lack of sugar. During Kellogg's annual convention at Key Biscayne in Florida, Leo was sitting by a swimming pool one evening surrounded by colleagues and clients. As usual, he was talking about advertising, strategy, and creativity. Suddenly, his voice choked and he passed out, his face resting on the table, mumbling: "Quick, a bar of chocolate." One of his colleagues hurried to a vending machine, knocking over some chairs. Leo feebly lifted his head and was able to shout: "And check that it's Nestlé!" demonstrating his total fidelity to his clients. Not only did Leo always buy one hundred shares in each company that became a new client, he also used nothing but their products: his pockets were always full of packets of Marlboro cigarettes, all his life he wore shoes made by the Brown Shoe Company, and until his death, Kellogg's Special K was on the table when he had breakfast. In 1967, with his health increasingly giving cause for concern, Leo, now seventy-six, decided reluctantly to give up the running of operations. That did not stop him from spending two long days at the agency every week, during which, using his famous

The image of the Marlboro cowboy was honed. The picture left is close to the definitive image which was immortalized by advertising.

black pencils

he would scribble enough pages of a notebook to fully occupy two hard-working secretaries. It was during this period, on December 1, 1967, during a breakfast attended by all the agency's employees, that he gave a speech that would be printed and distributed in all the branches under the title "When to Take My Name Off the Door": "Somewhere along the line, after I'm finally off the premises, you—or your successors—may want to take my name off the premises, too. You may want to call yourselves 'Twain, Rogers, Sawyer and Finn Inc.' . . . Or 'Ajax Advertising' or something. That will certainly be okay with me—if it's good for you . . . But let me tell you when I might demand that you take my name off the door. That will be the day when you spend more time trying to make money and less time making advertising—our kind of advertising. When you forget that the sheer fun of ad-making and the lift you get out of it—the creative climate of the place—should be as important as money to the very special breed of writers and artists and business professionals who compose this company of ours and make it tick. When you lose that restless feeling that nothing you do is ever quite good enough. When you lose your itch to do the job well for its own sake—regardless of the client, or the money, or the effort it takes. When you lose your passion for thoroughness . . . your hatred of loose ends. When you stop reaching for the manner, the overtone, the marriage of words and pictures that produces the fresh, the memorable and the believable effect. When you stop rededicating yourselves every day to the idea that better advertising is what the Leo Burnett Company is all about. When you are no longer what Thoreau called a 'corporation with a conscience'—which means to me, a corporation of conscientious men and women. When you begin to compromise your integrity—which has always been the heart's blood—the very guts of this agency. When you stoop to convenient expediency and rationalize yourselves into acts of opportunism—for the sake of a fast buck. When you show the slightest sign of crudeness, inappropriateness or smart-aleckness—and you lose that subtle sense of the fitness of things. When your main interest becomes a matter of size just to be big—rather than good, hard, wonderful work. When your outlook narrows down to the number of windows—from zero to five—in the walls of your office. When you lose your humility and become big-shot weisenheimers . . . a little too big for your boots. When the

apples come down to being just apples for eating (or for polishing)—no longer a part of our tone—our personality. When you disapprove of something, and start tearing the hell out of the man who did it, rather than the work itself. When you stop building on strong and vital ideas, and start a routine production line. When you start believing that, in the interest of efficiency, a creative spirit and the urge to create can be delegated and administered, and forget that they can only be nurtured, stimulated, and inspired. When you start giving lip service to this being a

creative

agency and stop really being one. Finally, when you lose your respect for the lonely man—the man at his typewriter or his drawing board or behind his camera or just

It had to be a child of Chicago,

scribbling notes with one of our big black pencils—or working all night on a media

that city of slaughterhouses, who

plan. When you forget that the lonely man—and thank God for him—has made the

promoted meat throughout

agency we now have possible. When you forget he's the man who, because he is

America.

reaching harder, sometimes actually gets hold of—for a moment—one of those hot, unreachable stars. That, boys and girls, is when I shall insist you take my name off the door. And by golly, it will be taken off the door. Even if I have to materialize long enough some night to rub it out myself—on every one of your floors. And before I dematerialize again, I will paint out that star-reaching symbol, too. And burn all the stationery. Perhaps tear up a few ads in passing. And throw every god-damned apple down the elevator shafts. You just won't know the place the next morning. You'll have to find another name." For some while, Leo had been in the habit of going to the horse races at Arlington, a racetrack near his home. During the season, he even went every Saturday. He claimed that it was an excellent way of not thinking about work: "You can't make an ad at a racetrack." He also spent more time giving interviews to the trade press, and the financial and business press. In 1970, during a long, eight-page interview in *Advertising Age*, he talked about many subjects. Among other things, he predicted the development of institutional adver-

tising. Asked also about the emergence of the young "rebel" agencies that will be discussed in the following chapters, Leo replied that there was, of course, room for these up-and-coming agencies, but that they should not attempt to make money too quickly. They should concentrate above all on building a solid foundation for their agencies, accepting lower profits and reinvesting continually. If they neglected to do this, he said, they would quickly burn themselves out. At the beginning of 1971, Leo Burnett Co. succeeded in launching Virginia Slims, a very slender cigarette aimed at women. The agency also acquired Dewar's whisky and launched Memorex audio cassettes, as well as Procter & Gamble's ERA detergent. In the mid-1960s, the agency became increasingly international, with a presence in

nineteen countries.

In 1968, business outside the United States was worth $85 million. This network was strengthened in 1970 with the opening of offices in Australia, New Zealand,

HE HATES CAVIAR, TOO!

Nothing fancy about him. He's just plain Bill. Honest, hardworking and happy with his three squares a day. But you'd never make him an honorary member of a gourmet society. Black olives, truffles, pâté de foie gras, venison? They're not part of his chow. So when it comes to beer, Guinness doesn't figure. The brisk, bright, not-quite-sweet, not-quite-sour, malty, winey flavor is wasted on him. But gourmets love it. It takes more than one hearing to enjoy Beethoven's Ninth. It takes more than one bottle to enjoy Guinness's Stout. But it's a pleasure that grows and grows. Isn't it significant that though very few like Guinness when they first try it, it's the world's largest beer export, now selling in a hundred and thirty-nine countries?

It is often said that one good picture is worth 10,000 words. That may be debatable—but not in this poster created by Leo Burnett for the *Daily News*. Everything can be understood at a glance.

DEWAR'S PROFILE:

MARK SALZMAN

HOME: Los Angeles, California.

AGE: 29.

PROFESSION: Author, actor, martial artist. "I know everyone in L.A. says that, but really, I am."

HOBBY: Going to the zoo. "It's the one place I won't be asked about China–except by, maybe, the pandas."

LAST BOOK READ: *Discos and Democracy: China in the Throes of Reform*, Orville Schell.

LATEST ACCOMPLISHMENT: Writing the script and starring in the movie "Iron and Silk," based on his book about his experiences as an English teacher in China.

WHY I DO WHAT I DO: "What else do you do with a degree from Yale in Chinese Language and Literature?"

QUOTE: 之呼者也

PROFILE: Animated, ebullient and prone to colorful exaggeration.

HIS SCOTCH: Dewar's® "White Label", straight up. "After years of drinking nothing but rice wine, it was a pleasure to return to a place where my Scotch was always on the menu."

White Label
DEWAR'S
BLENDED SCOTCH WHISKY
John Dewar & Sons
PERTH SCOTLAND

Thailand, Hong Kong, and Singapore. June 7, 1971, was one of the two days a week that Leo went to the agency. On that particular day, he sat there alone behind his large desk from where he could see Lake Michigan, an old man of seventy-nine at work, bathed in the afternoon sunlight. On his desk stood a glass apple, symbolizing all the red apples in all the Burnett agencies. To one side was a large pot containing the large black pencils that he liked. As usual, layouts were lying all over the sofa and

across the floor. When he left at the end of the day, Leo took a few files home with him, as he always did, so that he could look at them at his Lake Zurich property in the evening. He had a quiet dinner with his wife and died just as quietly during the night from a heart attack. Leo was dead, but not his work. Leo Burnett Co. continued to create strong, credible, and durable campaigns for brands such as United Airlines, Schlitz, and, above all, Marlboro and its cowboys. On August 5, 1985, for the agency's fiftieth anniversary, the agency was joined by all its old clients, as well as Wilson Sports Gear, Heinz, RCA, McDonald's, Beatrice Foods Food Trust, Hewlett Packard, Mars, and Seven-Up. The agency was present in thirty-two countries and employed 4,000 people, 2,300 outside the United States. The company as a whole was worth nearly $600 million. And traditions were maintained: in the reception of every Burnett agency stands a bowl of red apples—the Washington State Red variety—which are replaced every day. For twenty-five years, the same supplier has supplied the Chicago headquarters: Sam Houston and Son of Sutton Water Market Street. When the agency opened in 1935, eight apples were delivered every day; fifty years later the daily delivery was for 1,113 and took place between 7:00 and 8:00 A.M. The Burnett network uses 430,000 apples a year.

Different beer, different advertisement. Unrefined people may hate the Guinness, but everyone apparently likes the taste of Schlitz, an American beer in spite of its name.

An example, copied thousands of times since, of giving a product a cachet by associating it with a certain type of consumer. This was how Dewar's became famous in America.

bleustein-

Marcel Bleustein-Blanchet was the only French advertising pioneer who could be classified among the greatests. Unfortunately, or fortunately, he leaves the author of this book with little to say. Indeed, in three fat volumes—*La Rage de convaincre, Sur mon antenne, Ondes de la liberté*—Bleustein-Blanchet has written at length about himself and described in great detail the periods he lived through, the famous or quirky people he met on the way, and the products and services he successfully launched during his fruitful and obstinate sixty-year career. It only remains to summarize the basic facts and, more interestingly perhaps, to try to analyze this unusual person and exactly what he achieved. Marcel Bleustein-Blanchet was born in Enghien-les-Bains, France, on August 21, 1906. From an early age, he was in contact with business and sales, since his father, owner of a furniture store, dreamed of making young Marcel an outstanding furniture seller. Marcel was uninterested in his school studies and the only diploma he ever obtained was a "Certificat d'Etudes Primaires," the basic certificate

for finishing grammar school, which he continued proudly to include in the qualifications section in *Who's Who* and other yearbooks and directories devoted to the

He was the only Frenchman who

powerful and successful. And in spite of everything, it was business that gave him

could be classed among the great-

his vocation for advertising. Indeed, on the eve of his fifteenth birthday, he began

ests of his profession. It was he

working as a salesman in the family furniture store in the north of Paris. He became

who introduced modern advertis-

infected with the selling virus, taking pleasure in the challenge of finding the right

ing into France.

words to persuade people and trigger the buying impulse. But this enthusiasm for

blanchet

his work, this talent and vocation were to be channeled into an activity that was completely new to France: advertising. On May 30, 1927, at the age of twenty, he created "Publicis," a name composed of a shortening of the French word for advertising ("publicité"), and the number six. Why

"publicis"

and not "Publisept"? After all, although the idea for the project occurred to Marcel in 1926, it was only in 1927 that it got off the ground, but "Publicis" was more euphonic. So Marcel found himself in charge of a small company with capital of 50,000 francs, based in a small office at the end of a courtyard at 17, rue du Faubourg Montmartre. All he needed to do now was to find some clients. By chance, all the family's friends were in business, and they were naturally interested in anything that might improve sales. And as these people were friends, they were prepared to give the young Marcel a chance. The first to take the plunge would be Elie Berlin, the owner of the Comptoir Cardinet, which had never previously done any advertising. Thus the first advertisement by Publicis appeared just before Christmas 1927. It showed a thirty-two-piece tableware set and a clock, and included a special offer. The second advertiser to join Publicis, and another friend of the family, was Brunswick, the famous furrier on boulevard de Strasbourg. This advertisement featured Marcel's very first slogan: "Brunswick, le fourreur qui fait fureur!" ("Brunswick, the furrier who is all the rage!")

ore importantly, and more intelligently, Marcel spontaneously invented publicity mailing, sending a message written by the store owner to a list of potential clients. The agency's third client was both a friend of the family and a competitor: Lévitan. Once again, Bleustein-Blanchet composed a slogan: "Un meuble Lévitan est garanti pour longtemps." ("Lévitan furniture is guaranteed for a

long time.") These might seem absurdly

puerile today, but they must be seen in

the context of the period. Many of the

great popular stars of the time were

cabaret artists who always expressed

themselves in rhymes, and the slogans

used the same form, which also made

them easier to remember. It is worth not-

ing that, when it comes to being memo-

rable, the old slogans fared much better

than today's advertising jingles. In 1929,

Publicis moved to 62, boulevard de

Strasbourg, in a back room owned by its

client Brunswick. Bleustein-Blanchet

hired his first employees. Business must

have been going quite well at this time,

because he embarked on a tour of France

in a little airplane. The purpose of his

voyage had nothing to do with tourism

or gastronomy. In fact, Bleustein-

Blanchet had sensed that radio would be

an important medium for advertising. His aim was to set up agreements with the

largest number of radio stations possible. Barely twenty-three, he thus became the

exclusive vendor of radio advertising, for both state and private stations. This stroke of

genius provided much more in the way of income than the actual activities of the

agency, which was still in its infancy. It was around this time that, thanks to a shared

interest in flying, Bleustein-Blanchet acquired his fourth client and his biggest account.

andré shoes,

who invested 600,000 francs, were undergoing rapid expansion thanks to radio, which ensured national coverage. They were joined by Banania, Francorusse, Floraline, Gemey, Max Factor, Monsavon, Rivoire Carret, Marie-Rose, and Solls, who were attracted by the personality of Bleustein-Blanchet and the possibilities offered by radio advertising. In 1932, expansion forced Publicis to move again. But this time they were not at the end of a courtyard, nor in a back room, but at 1, boulevard Haussmann, today the headquarters of the Banque Nationale de Paris. The name "Publicis" appeared on the façade.

In 1934, the French government under Georges Mandel introduced the radio license, with the result that advertising on state radio stations was forbidden. For Bleustein-Blanchet, this measure led to the abrupt loss of twelve million francs worth of radio advertising contracts. Undeterred, he decided to set up his own radio station. He bought up Radio LL, which he immediately renamed Radio-Cité. Thanks to his experience in the medium, his knowledge of popular taste and his flair for presenting information, he was able to make Radio-Cité the second most important radio station in France. The station was innovative and combined all the elements needed for success: live public shows, radio games, the first hourly news program (produced in collaboration with journalists from *L'Intransigeant*), with special news flashes for important events, and advertisements sung by cabaret singers or newcomers, who included Charles Trenet. Advertisers could also sponsor live shows by inviting their clients and their employees. Radio-Crochet, recorded in the Salle Pleyel, and the programs of Jean Nohain, Mireille, and Saint-Granier were enormous successes. An idea as good as this one was worth applying elsewhere, and that was what Bleustein-Blanchet did. First, he created the Ecrans de Publicis, a company with the aim of developing advertising in movie theaters, then in 1935 he joined Léon Régnier, CEO of Havas, to create Cinéma et Publicité, which today is the largest agency handling cinema advertising in France. In 1938, Bleustein-Blanchet did the same thing for the press when he founded Régie Presse, set up to

André shoes—Publicis' fourth advertiser. A budget of 600,000 francs and a strong radio presence led to spectacular growth.

handle advertising space in newspapers and magazines. The same year, he went on a study trip to America, bringing back to France new techniques and methods. In America, he discovered market studies, motivation studies, and, after a meeting with George Gallup, opinion polls. He promoted their use in France and convinced Pierre Mendès-France to use opinion polls in 1954 to find out about French attitudes toward politics and politicians. On the eve of World War II, Bleustein-Blanchet's agency was simultaneously a consultancy, an agency managing press, radio, and cinema advertising, and a medium in the form of Radio-Cité. He was rich and powerful. He was thirty-two years old. But the war and the Occupation swept everything away. Sought both by the Vichy police and the Gestapo, Blanchet-Bleustein fled France and reached England via Spain. There he joined the Forces Aériennes Françaises Libres as a pilot. After the Liberation, he was awarded the Croix de Guerre with Palmes and Etoile d'Argent, the Médaille de la Résistance, the Médaille de l'Aéronautique, and the Légion d'Honneur, but he was bankrupt. Together with his former colleagues and a few new ones, on January 1, 1946, he started again

from scratch.

This time, there was no possibility of using radio—all the stations were nationalized and

ROSY
a le secret des formes

advertising was forbidden—so Bleustein-Blanchet concentrated on activities of Publicis. His former clients gradually returned, as and when they were able to advertise, notably André, Lévitan, Brunswick, Comptoir Cardinet, and Bouchara. In 1947, they were joined by Colgate Palmolive and Rosy, and in 1948 by Prénatal, Corot, Weil, Primior, and Gringoire. Bleustein-Blanchet then returned to the United States to assess how communications techniques had evolved. As a result, his agency started using campaign plans, market studies, and motivation studies. He set up an agreement with the IFOP (Institut d'Opinion Public Français), and in 1948 created a study and research department. He was also the first person to bring the father of motivational research, Ernest Dichter, over from the United States. In 1949, Publicis linked up with Métrobus, the advertising sales agency for the Paris subway and bus network. Cinéma et Publicité prospered and, as one never disowns one's first love, Bleustein-Blanchet joined up with Régie No. 1, the advertising sales agency of the radio station Europe No. 1. More new clients followed: Singer in 1950 and the Sopad Nestlé group in 1952. Publicis was given an Oscar for its advertising for Shell. In 1957, Marcel Bleustein-Blanchet realized a dream from his working-class childhood: he reigned over the Champs-Elysées and was able to look out on the Arc de Triomphe. Publicis moved into premises at number 133 on the Champs-Elysées in a building known as the Shape, which had previously housed the Hôtel Astoria and had served as the headquarters of the Allied Forces. The owner of the building was Emile Jellineck—father, promoter, and ambassador of Mercedes. In April 1958, Bleustein-Blanchet began to branch out into retail, ignoring the advice of everybody, to create the very first Drugstore Publicis. It stayed open until 2:00 A.M. and offered a wide variety of services. It was an immediate success, becoming a popular place for young people to hang out. In 1959, Publicis created the Business Information Section, which was the first incarnation of the Business Communication Organization, one of whose client's was Lip. After this, a succession of clients arrived, some unknown at the time, others important: Caisse d'Epargne, Tapis Sommer, Dim (then known as Bas

There was disagreement over who exactly created this campaign, but it was widely admired. One thing is for sure: it was by Publicis and it went down in the history of advertising as, among other things, the first ad not to show the product.

Dimanche), the SCAD, Flodor, Renault, and Boursin, an unknown company new to advertising with a tiny budget of 300,000 francs. This period of rapid growth culminated in Publicis being floated on the French stock market in 1970. On September 27, 1972, an enormous fire destroyed the Publicis building in one night, but Bleustein-Blanchet carried on, surrounded by his loyal colleagues and clients. Bleustein-Blanchet eventually handed the reins of the company over to Maurice Lévy in 1985. Lévy became vice-president of the group. He had overall control and was responsible for directing international operations. Bleustein-Blanchet himself was becoming increasingly hard of hearing, a handicap which forced him to entrust more and more of his clients to his successor. Two years later, the father of Publicis decided to hand over all responsibil-

ities for good, even though he continued to

go to the office every day until he died.

Marcel Bleustein-Blanchet invited his spiritu-

al son over to inform him of his decision to

change the structure of Publicis. In 1987,

Publicis became a company with a board of

directors, and a supervisory board directed

by Bleustein-Blanchet. He entrusted his daughter Elisabeth Badinter with looking after and safeguarding the company's heritage. Although Lévy and Bleustein-Blanchet had an excellent understanding, they were not always in agreement about the correct strategy to adopt. When the new president of the board saw the early signs of globalization, and realized the necessity for the agency to develop internationally, Bleustein replied, "I understand why we need to be present in the United States, but as for the other countries, what's the point?" In spite of this reluctance, the father of the company listened to the son and the conquest of new territories began. In 1988, Publicis became the principal shareholder of the group F.C.B., managed at the time by Norman Brown. The partnership worked well until 1992, when Brown retired. Then war broke out with Bruce Mason, new president of F.C.B., who was intent on ending the merger. "Mason could not bear Publicis having control of F.C.B.'s activities in Europe," explained

maurice lévy.

Mason and the F.C.B. board created a new company in 1994, True North Communications, and there followed a year-long fight between Publicis and True North, leading to the dissolution of their partnership in 1996. A few weeks after the break up of Publicis and True North, on February 29, 1996, Marcel Bleustein-Blanchet died. This was a blow not only to his children, but also to Maurice Lévy. The latter recalled with humor and emotion their last "Jewish joke," their final "victory": "Monsignor Lustiger called me to warn me that Publicis was in competition with Eurocom and BDDP to organize the World Youth Days. When I told Marcel the news, he was like a kid: 'This is our Légion d'Honneur. We must have this account.' Meanwhile, Marcel had fallen ill and each time he was able, he asked me about Maurice and the campaign for the archbishop. On April 10, in the evening, I called him, still with no news, and he repeated, 'Well, what about the pope, have we had an answer? We must win. You must give me this satisfaction.' That was our last conver-

Publicis turned Bas Dimanche stockings into Dim stockings. First there were the stockings sold for one franc, then the ten stockings for ten francs, and finally the famous Dim panty hose at a time when dresses and skirts were getting more and more mini.

LES CHIPS FLODOR... BLONDES A CROQUER !

sation. He fell asleep and did not wake up. On April 17, seven days after his death, Monsignor Lustiger contacted me. 'I was about to call you when I heard of M. Bleustein-Blanchet's death, so I allowed eight days of mourning to pass before announcing that you had won.' I found it very awkward." In the end, Publicis won. "Marcel must have been happy," added Maurice Lévy, "because there had never been such a successful event." Bleustein-Blanchet died just as true globalization was beginning for Publicis. Maurice Lévy traveled the world and established the agency's name in thirty-six new countries, beginning with Mexico, Brazil, Canada, and Singapore. Last but not least, the president oversaw the acquisition of Saatchi & Saatchi in 2000. Publicis is now the fifth largest communications group in the world, and is present in 100 countries and 165 cities, with a total of 18,000 employees. There have been a number of important new clients, including British Airways and Hewlett-Packard. Lévy also won Coca-Cola in his own inimitable style. The soft drinks giant parted company with the agency McCann-Erikson in 1997 and had decided to place its future in the hands of the agency CAA. Lévy sent a congratulatory letter to the marketing director

How do you turn a potato chip

of Coca-Cola, the content of which could be summarized as follows: "Congratulations

into a glamorous delicacy, worthy

for choosing CAA. You are the first marketing director crazy enough to choose a

of refined places and people?

Hollywood agency. But are you crazy enough to work with a French agency?" There

Just ask Publicis. That's what

was no answer, so Lévy sent another letter. "I do not know if you are crazy enough,

Flodor did in 1959. Art direction

but you are certainly not polite enough . . ." Today, Publicis handles advertising for

was by Jean Feldman, a gentle-

Coca-Cola in forty different countries—something that would no doubt have delighted

man who preferred blondes.

the man who made it possible for the empire to prosper after his death.

BLONDE
A
CROQUE
?

ogilvy

avid Ogilvy, a very English Englishman, was like a man from another world in America. With his tweed suits, his collection of pipes, his snobbery, and his very British outlook, many would agree that Ogilvy was one of the most extraordinary characters in the history of advertising. Despite his fascination for America and the fact that he lived there for most of his life, for Americans Ogilvy remained a "British guy." He was born the fourth of five children in West Horsley near London on June 23, 1911, to an Irish mother and a Scottish father, neither of whom showed much affection. Dominated by an elder brother, apparently gifted at everything, but incapable of identifying with his father, the young David was a shy child. Later on, many years of psychoanalysis revealed that he was suffering from a problem of masculine identity. When he was eight, he was sent to boarding school. He missed his family terribly and was deeply unhappy.

He read *Huckleberry Finn* and started to dream of America. He eventually won a scholarship to Oxford, but was expelled soon after because of his poor results.

Despite his family's objections, and without his father's help, he obtained a post in the kitchens of the Majestic, a large hotel in Paris. He worked sixty-five hours a week for a ridiculous salary. Even so, the experience left him with happy memories and a thousand anecdotes, and he later went so far as to claim that what he learned at the Majestic was of use to him throughout his career. His family eventually insisted on his coming home and he went off to do door-to-door selling in Scotland for Aga Cookers. He did well and even wrote a guide for Aga salesmen, which

earned him a job with the advertising agency Mather & Crowther, where his brilliant brother was head of advertising. At the age of nearly twenty-five, and without knowing it yet, he had just found his vocation. He read everything he could find on the subject and worked every night until 3:00 A.M. He subscribed to a Chicago clipping service that sent him the new campaigns. He implored

mather & crowther

to send him to the United States to study new advertising techniques, and they agreed. At the same time, he asked NBC to teach him about new radio advertising techniques. He was recommended to NBC's New York correspondent, and the little boy who dreamed of America while reading *Huckleberry Finn* discovered the skyscrapers of Manhattan at the age of twenty-seven. His work for NBC enabled him to see shows and rehearsals, and to meet advertising executives. He was crazy about the campaigns of Young and Rubicam, particularly the one for Sanka coffee. In what proved to be one of the key encounters of his life, he met Rosser Reeves, who at the time was a freelance copywriter and disciple of Claude Hopkins. The two men started having lunch together. Ogilvy was disconcerted, shaken by Rosser Reeves' theories, and the latter was no doubt astonished and charmed by the young David, who ended up marrying the sister of Rosser's wife.

avid decided to settle in the United States and worked for three years for George Gallup's Audience Research Group. He dealt with more than four hundred opinion polls and studies. He liked the scientific approach of the studies and found them reassuring. Indeed, the rigorous, technical approach adopted in the studies became a feature of his work. After completing his military service at the British Embassy in Washington, Ogilvy had the opportunity of traveling to see the Amish. He found their nineteenth-century way of life rather appeal

ing, in particular the sense of security and continuity it provided. He described these years as the richest of his life. He settled with his wife and son in a farm in Lancaster County and, in keeping with the sect's customs, grew a long beard and traveled by mule to work in his tobacco fields. If he had been stronger and less clumsy, and if he had been more at ease with animals, Manhattan would never have heard of David Ogilvy. But he returned to the advertising world. He was very attracted by Young and Rubicam of course, but was sure that after ten years' absence from advertising they would not hire him. Consequently, he decided to open his own agency. He put his savings of $6,000 into it and obtained financial backing from Mather & Crowther and another London agency, Benson Ltd. It was the first British agency in New York. The chairman was not Ogilvy, however. For that post, a man named Anderson Hewitt was hired, with Ogilvy as vice chairman, in charge of studies and research. Thus, in September 1948, the agency Hewitt, Ogilvy, Benson & Mather went into business, with a few small British accounts, including Guinness. In 1951, the agency acquired its first American client: a little clothing firm from Maine:

hathaway.

This provided David Ogilvy with the opportunity to adopt a new approach. He proposed that the shirts, which were rather cheap, be sold as if they were luxury articles. He set about creating a sense of sophistication. The agency selected a model of about fifty, with gray hair and a respectable mustache. For good measure, the character was given a black patch over one eye, a detail which derived from two memories Ogilvy had: one of a former teacher, the other of a photo of the American ambassador to Great Britain. The "man in the Hathaway shirt" appeared for the first time in *The New Yorker* on September 22, 1951. Sales rocketed. The man in the Hathaway shirt went on to appear in numerous situations: buying a $2,000

The ship you see is the *Carinthia*, Cunard Steam-Ship Company Limi[

Unloading Schweppes elixir on Pier 92

ABOVE YOU SEE Commander Edward Whitehead, President of Schweppes U.S.A., welcoming still another cargo of Schweppes elixir to America.

The Commander imports this precious essence from England, to make sure that every drop of Schweppes Tonic bottled in America has the *original* flavor. The *curiously refreshing* flavor that has made Schweppes famous all over the world as the authentic Gin-and-Tonic mixer.

Says Commander Whitehead: "It took the House of Schweppes more than a century to bring Schweppes Tonic to its bittersweet perfection. And to develop Schweppervescence— patrician little bubbles that always *last your whole drink through*."

But it will take *you* only seconds to mix Gin or Vodka with Schweppes and enjoy the delicious results.

P.S. Add this new drink to your Schweppertory: a jigger of Dry Vermouth over ice and Schweppes Tonic. Tastes almost like champagne!

Purdey rifle, painting a picture, conducting a symphony orchestra. The text for each advertisement consisted of five paragraphs outlining and explaining each selling point. In August 1952, David Ogilvy was fortunate enough to spend a weekend with Ray Rubicam. Rubicam spoke with Ogilvy at great length, answered his questions and gave him advice. Ogilvy took Rubicam as his role model, and Rubicam corresponded with his young disciple for five years. But becoming a follower of Rubicam meant giving up the theories of Hopkins and his successor Rosser Reeves, which was not an easy thing for Ogilvy to do. He thought and tried to act like Rubicam. Rubicam told him that an agency should only be run by a single man, so Ogilvy parted company with Anderson Hewitt, just as Rubicam had separated from Young, and the agency was renamed Ogilvy, Benson and Mather. The company's second success came, once again, with another image campaign. Mather & Crowther sent the account for

schweppes

quinine water from London. Ogilvy found the $15,000 budget too small and, moreover, thought the product did not have a future, so he turned it down. His London associates insisted, however. They suggested that the chairman of Schweppes himself could be used for the photo. Commander Edward Whitehead did have a rather extraordinary face for the American public. Americans tended to be clean-shaven or have short, inconspicuous beards, but Whitehead sported an enormous bushy beard. Once again, the image was intriguing. Who was it? Why did he have such a distinctive beard? Where was he from? It made Schweppes, which some people had described as barely drinkable, a success. After the Hathaway man came the Schweppes man. Ogilvy's agency, which was supposed to be founded on the bedrock of research and based on the theories of Hopkins, had suddenly acquired the reputation of being very creative. Ogilvy, repudiating Rosser Reeves' doctrine

Commander Whitehead, the "real" chairman of Schweppes, was another character to emerge from the Ogilvy agency.

Hathaway's new "Suburban"—the informal shirt that <u>fits</u>

HATHAWAY designed the *Suburban* shirt for weekends. But lately we have noticed it's been turning up *in town*—particularly on Monday mornings.

Some men just can't bear to be parted from a shirt that combines the *comfort* of a sports shirt with the *trimness* of a business shirt. And you can't blame them. The

Suburban is informal—but it fits. It comes in exact neck and sleeve sizes—and it also has those generous Hathaway tails that stay inside your trousers.

Notice the button-down collar too. It is "banded," so it takes a tie. Which is a mercy, since as everyone already knows, "If you don't wear a collar and a tie, you

won't go to heaven when you die."

You can get these versatile *Suburban* shirts in sixty of Hathaway's most interesting fabrics. The shirt in our picture is an imported English gingham—at $8.95.

For the name of your nearest store, write C. F. Hathaway, Waterville, Maine —or call OXford 7-5566 in New York.

and making Rubicam his idol, abandoned polls and qualitative studies to devote himself to creativity and copywriting. He was barely forty years old. Stanley Resor, the chairman of J. Walter Thompson, even tried to hire him. His reputation as a creative person astonished his brothers and sisters, because it did not correspond to their image of him. He worked seven days a week. At the office, he dealt with administrative problems, attended meetings, and generally ran the agency. But everything to do with thinking and copywriting he did at home.

his colleagues remember Ogilvy as being rather formal and not particularly warm. Every new employee was required to learn by heart the Ogilvy rules and to obey them strictly. The principal rules: always include the brand name in the heading; do not try to be clever or smart; do not use analogies; avoid superlatives; use sentences of less than twelve words; do not make jokes; and use photographs instead of artwork where possible. This strict imposition of rules could frustrate many people, hampering creativity and leading to over-rigid campaigns, but clients loved it. For them, the reliance on rules provided a reassuring element of certainty, a scientific approach. David Ogilvy excelled at dealing with clients. Many said that he was a better businessman and salesman of his creations than he was a creative person, in the strict sense of the term. And yet Ogilvy wrote many advertisements. He never got carried away by his imagination or his intuitions, however. As a precaution, he studied the whole file, examined the campaigns of his competitors, questioned the market research department at length, drew up a list of facts and arguments, and set down the sales problem, the aims of the campaign, and the arguments that needed to be emphasized to the client to sell it to him. It was only then that he attempted to write a heading—and even then he would think up more than twenty for a single advertisement. The blank page caused him anguish. Ideas came to him very laboriously. Despite living for twenty years in

The eye-catching man with the black eye patch was created by David Ogilvy. It turned a small manufacturer from Maine into a legendary brand.

America, Ogilvy still spoke the English of his country of birth and took tea every day in his office at 4:30 P.M. exactly. He sported a tweed suit, silk twill handkerchiefs in his breast pocket, and filled his pipes with a special blend from London. He enjoyed listening to Bach, Handel, and Mozart, as well as military music from time to time. He preferred the company of writers and intellectuals to that of colleagues. He was the kind of person who impressed his advertisers, who were for the most part self-made men who lacked his affectations and sophisticated manners. And yet Ogilvy did not read much except for magazines, the *Reader's Digest* in particular, no doubt for advertising reasons. He used, in speech and in his advertisements, words which seemed supremely elegant to him, but which he was incapable of defining, such as "ineffably." He eventually admitted to having a mediocre mastery of English.

espite all his success and awards, he was regarded in the profession as an eccentric Englishman only capable of creating sophisticated campaigns designed to appear in *The New Yorker*. And yet others started to copy him. In 1953, five years after the agency was founded, business reached nearly $11 million. In 1954, the figure dropped, then increased by $4 million for the following two years. Big companies seemed immune to the rules and creative approach of Ogilvy. But in 1956, he had the good idea of hiring Esty Stowell as sales manager. Stowell came from Benton & Bowles and his role was to give Ogilvy, Benson & Mather a more muscular image thanks to his experience of hard selling and his reputation as a hard-hitting salesman. Stowell worked wonders, getting among others Maxwell House coffee, the agency's first large account. In 1957, when

rolls-royce

offered its account to Ogilvy, Stowell suggested they turn them down on the grounds that it would reinforce the agency's elitist image, which was off-putting to big clients. But Ogilvy was keen to have the account, because, among other reasons, Rolls-Royce had been with Young & Rubicam some years before. Ogilvy started work on the campaign alone. For four days, he got up at 5:00 A.M. to write.

f the twenty-six headings that he proposed, his associates chose only one: "At 60 miles an hour the loudest noise in this new Rolls-Royce comes from the electric clock." Incidentally, this was almost identical to the heading used in an ad written in 1933 for Pierce Arrow by the agency BBDO. As was his custom, under this heading Ogilvy wrote a long text, full of explanations and statistics. This was the agency's third big success of this kind in seven years. But, as with Hathaway and Schweppes, the Rolls-Royce campaign made money for the client, but not for the agency. Ogilvy himself looked after the "poor" accounts, leaving his colleagues to work for the big clients, who were less receptive to this form of communication.

Once again, as always in this profession, a dilemma between the size of the agency and the quality of its work arose. Meanwhile, Rosser Reeves, the guru rejected by Ogilvy, the champion of hard selling, had led the Bates agency from billings of $29 million to $103 million. No doubt impressed by this success, Ogilvy approached Reeves and the two made up in 1959. After an aborted merger

Still under the aegis of Commander Whitehead, Schweppes continued its campaign with a small budget. Thanks to Ogilvy's talent, this beverage scorned by Americans became the star of every party.

"*Schweppes is the only mixer for an authentic Gin-and-Tonic!*" insists Commander Whitehead.

The President of Schweppes U.S.A. tells why nobody has ever been able to imitate the famous _flavor_ of Schweppes Tonic

THE House of Schweppes makes the *authentic* Tonic mixer. Schweppes has been famous all over the world since 1794. Yet nobody, anywhere, has been able to imitate Schweppes thirst-quenching, bittersweet *flavor*.
Every bottle of Schweppes Tonic, no matter *where* in the world it is bottled,

starts with a unique elixir imported from London, England.
The formula for this elixir is known to only three living men, and calls for a secret blend of exotic ingredients.
"The water used in making Schweppes Tonic is purified to an obsessive degree," says Commander Edward Whitehead, President of

Schweppes U.S.A. "Crystal clear, *extra pure* water is one of the secrets of Schw<u>pp</u>ervescence—little bubbles that *last your whole drink through.*"
Whether you drink Gin-and-Tonic, Vodka-and-Tonic, Rum-and-Tonic, or just plain Tonic—make sure the barman brings you *Schweppes*.
Curiously refreshing!

The Rolls-Royce Silver Cloud II—$15,6...

"At 60 miles an hour the loudest noise in this new Rolls-Royce comes from the electric clock"

What __makes__ Rolls-Royce the best car in the world? "There is really no magic about it—it is merely patient attention to detail," says an eminent Rolls-Royce engineer.

1. "At 60 miles an hour the loudest noise comes from the electric clock," reports the Technical Editor of THE MOTOR. The silence of the engine is uncanny. Three mufflers tune out sound frequencies—acoustically.

2. Every Rolls-Royce engine is run for seven hours at full throttle before installation, and each car is test-driven for hundreds of miles over varying road surfaces.

3. The Rolls-Royce Silver Cloud II is designed as an *owner-driven* car. It is eighteen inches shorter than the largest domestic cars.

4. The car has power steering, power brakes and automatic gear-shift. It is very easy to drive and to park. No chauffeur required.

5. There is no metal-to-metal contact between the body of the car and the chassis frame—except for the speedometer drive. The entire body is insulated and under-sealed.

6. The finished car spends a week in the final test-shop, being fine-tuned.

Here it is subjected to ninety-eight separate ordeals. For example, the engineers use a *stethoscope* to listen for axle-whine.

7. The new eight-cylinder aluminium engine is even more *powerful* than the previous six-cylinder unit, *yet it weighs ten pounds less.*

8. The famous Rolls-Royce radiator has never been changed, except that when Sir Henry Royce died in 1933 the monogram RR was changed from red to black.

9. The coachwork is given five coats of primer paint, and hand rubbed between each coat, before *nine* coats of finishing paint go on.

10. By moving a switch on the steering column, you can adjust the shock-absorbers to suit road conditions. (The lack of fatigue in driving this car is remarkable.)

11. Another switch defrosts the rear window, by heating a network of 1360 invisible wires in the glass. The ventilating system is so efficient that you

can ride in comfort with all the windows closed. Air conditioning is optional.

12. The seats are upholstered with eight hides of English leather—enough to make 128 pairs of soft shoes.

13. A picnic table, veneered in French walnut, slides out from under the dash. Two more swing out behind the front seats.

14. You can get such optional extras as an Espresso coffee-making machine, a dictating machine, a bed, hot and cold water for washing, an electric razor.

15. The cooling fan is *lopsided*. Its five blades are unequally spaced and pitched to take thick and thin slices of air. Thus it does its work in a *whisper*. The company goes to fantastic lengths to ensure the peace and quiet of the occupants of the car.

16. There are *three* independent brake linkages. The Rolls-Royce is a very *safe* car—and also a very *lively* car. It cruises serenely at eighty-five. Top speed is in excess of 100 m.p.h.

17. Rolls-Royce engineers make periodic visits to inspect owners' motor cars and advise on service.

18. The Bentley is made by Rolls-Royce. Except for the radiators, they are identical motor cars, manufactured by the same engineers in the same works. The Bentley costs $300 less, because its radiator is simpler to make. People who feel diffident about driving a Rolls-Royce can buy a Bentley.

ROLLS-ROYCE AND BENTLEY

PRICE. The car illustrated in this advertisement — f.o.b. principal port of entry—costs **$15,655.**

If you would like the rewarding experience of driving a Rolls-Royce or Bentley, write or telephone dealer listed below. Rolls-Royce Inc., 45 Rockefeller Plaza, New York 20, N.Y.

project with Leo Burnett in 1955, David Ogilvy went from strength to strength, and

succeeded in transforming his "creative boutique" into one of the top ten agencies.

In 1960, Shell left J. Walter Thompson, handing Ogilvy its account of nearly $13

million. This almost doubled the agency's business and Ogilvy opened an office in

Toronto so that he could handle Shell in Canada as well. In the following years,

Sears, KLM, American Express, and IBM entrusted the agency with their accounts.

All the clients paid the agency fees instead of the usual deal of 15%.

In the summer of 1962, Ogilvy spent his vacation writing a book, in which he set

out his theories and illustrated them with anecdotes drawn from his experiences.

No doubt frightened by the consequences of his indiscretions, he finally decided to

delete the gossip and anecdotes from the manuscript before sending it to his pub-

lisher. Ogilvy was expecting modest sales of 5,000 copies, but 400,000 copies were

sold in five years and more than one million in twenty years. *Confessions of an*

Advertising Man was structured pragmatically around the various questions which

were at the heart of advertising: How do you run an agency? How do you get

clients and keep them? How do you advertise efficiently? In the book's sixteen

chapters, Ogilvy set out what amounted to the catechism of advertising, accompa-

nied of course by illustrations taken from the work of the evangelist himself. One

Opposite: This is probably Ogilvy's best-known ad. It was chosen from 26 different ads created over a four-day period of ten-hour days. Above: Ray Rubicam, another advertising great, and founder of Young and Rubicam, was in charge of the Rolls-Royce account before it went to Ogilvy.

day, he was asked why he had written this book and he replied, half joking and half cynically, "I liked the idea of people spending $5 on a presentation of my agency." It must have been a success, because shortly after the book appeared, the agency's business, which had been $58 million, rose to $77 million in 1964. From this time on, describing himself as an

"extinct volcano,"

he wrote fewer and fewer campaigns. In 1965, merger with Mather & Crowther led to the creation of Ogilvy & Mather in London. At the same time, Ogilvy, weary of advertising, moved to a château near Tours, in France. He was only fifty when he made this decision to retire from the profession. This early retirement did not stop this giant of advertising from supervising the future of his agency from a distance, although he never actually got involved directly. As he lived in France, he occasionally sent messages to the Paris office. So it was as an active observer that Ogilvy saw his agency become part of WPP, the leading communications group in the world, following a hostile takeover bid by the latter in 1989. The operation took the agency created by David Ogilvy to seventh place in the world, with 377 offices in 97 countries, 10,000 employees and 1,500 clients. And yet, surprisingly, Ogilvy & Mather has succeeded in retaining its identity. The man who above all liked to describe himself as a copywriter wanted to create a worldwide network with strong local agencies—agencies that did more than merely adapt campaigns from neighboring agencies, agencies that would respect the culture of the target public. Ogilvy was keen to define the precepts that underpinned his approach. The key sentences are all preserved in the books he wrote and in the company brochures. He had humorously referred to these precepts as

"magic lanterns."

In fact, these were the group's strong points and they were recorded in a small, prac-

tical book that everyone could consult. In its various chapters, copywriters or sales people could find out how to address children, how to fight Procter, or how to do advertising for tourism. David Ogilvy valued efficiency above all else, and hated gratuitous creative work and pointless fireworks. In an interview given in 1991, he described advertising awards as a plague on the profession. Two days later, the famous French ad "La Lionne," made by Jean-Paul Goude and the French agency for Perrier, won the Grand Prix at the Festival International de la Publicité which is held in Cannes. This most prestigious of prizes, the one everyone in the profession dreams of winning throughout the year, nearly slipped through Ogilvy's fingers. The festival organizer, Roger Hatchuel, was so angry about his remarks that he did not want to award him the prize. In the end, the two men talked things through and the ceremony proceeded without a hitch. David Ogilvy died on July 22, 1999. On July 23, in the French newspaper *Le Monde*, his photo was printed along with the sentence that he wanted to see printed on his death: "I'd like to be remembered as a copywriter who had some big ideas."

Beer and oysters! Here, the British duo of Guinness and Ogilvy provides a consumer's guide to oysters.

bernbach

ne day in June 1949, three men opened a new agency in the heart of Manhattan with thirteen employees and business of $500,000. The agency was located at 350 Madison Avenue. To reach the offices, you had to take the elevator to the top and then walk up a further story. The first of these three men was Ned Doyle, forty-seven years old, who was in charge of sales. He had started out in magazine sales and advertising, before working as head of sales in an agency. The second man was Maxwell Dane, forty-three years old, who was in charge of administration and finances. He and Doyle had met ten years before when Dane was promotion director of the magazine *Look*. As suave and discreet as Doyle was brusque and assertive, Dane was like an archetypal financial manager and kept a low profile. The third man was William Bernbach. He also looked like an accountant or professor, but he was the creative soul of the agency. In this month of June 1949, nobody yet knew that this new agency, which was simply called Doyle, Dane, Bernbach, would become one of the brightest stars in the advertising firmament and would serve as a school for a generation of professionals who would spearhead the "creative revolution" in American advertising. The man responsible for this was Bill Bernbach. He invented a new style of advertising, and attracted and trained a host of talented people from the end of the 1950s to the end of the 1960s. Bernbach was born in the Bronx in 1921. His father designed women's clothes. After completing his schooling, Bernbach went to New York University every day by subway, where he studied English, music, and philosophy, displaying even at this early stage the breadth of interests that would serve him

He revolutionized the style of advertising, he inspired the most brilliant campaigns, and he attracted and trained the most gifted people, people who continue to demonstrate their talent in advertising today, but Bernbach, unlike others, was incapable, or unwilling, of creating an empire.

so well later on in advertising. In 1932, he began working as an office boy for Schenley Distillers Company, subsequently moving into the advertising department. In 1939, he left Schenley to work as a ghostwriter for Grover Whalen, who was the head of the 1939 World's Fair in New York. After the fair, he heard about an opening with the William H.

weintraub

advertising agency. He began working as a copywriter, working with the graphic designer Paul Rand on the Dubonnet and Air-Wick accounts. During their lunch hour, they would visit art galleries together and discuss the interplay of words and images. In 1945, Bill Bernbach joined Grey Advertising, where he worked closely with Bob Gage. On the day of their first meeting, Gage said to his wife when he came home that evening that someday he would go into business with Bernbach because "I understood what he was talking about and he understood me." Together they worked on numerous campaigns for shirts, watches, alcoholic beverages, fashion, and even for discount stores on Seventh Avenue. The latter provided a special kind of training. These accounts required great speed, intense work, and immediate, concrete results in terms of sales. Having quickly risen to the position of copy chief at Grey, Bill Bernbach received a lot of résumés and interviewed an enormous number of candidates. Yet he was perturbed to discover that most "creative" people were too easily influenced by the fashion for pseudo-scientific techniques.

I n 1947, Bernbach wrote a long memo to his superiors, developing the themes which were dear to him and which would form his creed throughout his career. "I'm worried that we're going to fall into the trap of bigness, that we're going to worship techniques instead of substance," he wrote. "I don't want academicians. I don't want scientists. I don't want people who do the right things. I want people who do inspiring things. . . . Let us blaze new trails." This memo apparently had little effect, which turned out to be a good thing, for if it had Bernbach might have become a director at Grey, DDB would not have existed, and the face of advertising would not have been changed for good. DDB took off at the beginning of the 1950s, shortly after the agency had moved to a modest building on

west 3rd street.

Although the agency grew quickly and went from success to success, the office decor was always very plain—unlike other agencies, DDB never sought to impress their clients through sumptuous premises. Graphic designers and copywriters worked in

"Liberal Trade-In: bring in your wife and just a few dollars . . . we will give you a new woman." This ad marked a radical change in the way big stores advertised.

teams on the same floor. Doyle and Dane lived in ordinary apartments in Manhattan, while Bernbach, a committed subway user, lived in a small house in Brooklyn. "We probably do less entertaining than any agency in the business," explained Bernbach. "We're three guys who live very modestly and we don't cater to clients because we want the money." That sums up in a nutshell both the agency's philosophy and Bernbach's personality. His appearance was, indeed, unassuming. Anyone shown a photograph of this man and asked his profession would be more likely to reply "history professor" or "accountant" rather than "advertising executive."

h e wore dark suits, white shirts, and sober ties. The look in his blue eyes expressed a well-balanced and self-confident personality. Bernbach boasted that he never worked late at night or weekends, and never took work home in the evening. He worked hard during the day, then took the Sea Beach Express home. Uninterested in sports, he spent his free time listening to music and reading. His interests ranged from novels to philosophy and sociology. And yet this modest-looking man, with his straightforward life, created or inspired the largest number of immortal campaigns in the history of advertising. He was the catalyst for a whole generation of brilliant and talented people, the inventor a new form of advertising. After him, advertising would never

You don't have to be Jewish

to love Levy's
real Jewish Rye

be the same. He had more imagination and humor than those members of his profession who dressed eccentrically and lived flamboyant lives.

But beneath this modest façade, it would be unwise to underestimate Bill Bernbach's ego, as many anecdotes about him testify. One day, for example, Bernbach took the elevator with one of his clients to accompany him back to the lobby. When they reached the door, the client looked out and said, "What wonderful weather!" And Bernbach simply replied, "Thank you!" Bernbach had one peculiar habit: such was his self-confidence that he always carried in his pocket a small card on which a sentence was printed. When he received someone in his office, he would take the card out of his pocket and put it in front of him. On this card was written: "Be careful, maybe he is right!" This character trait was confirmed by David Ogilvy, who said that it was impossible to lunch with Bernbach without receiving a lesson in advertising, as if one was a young intern in his office. Every campaign went through Bernbach's office, but unlike Burnett he supervised with a light touch and great sensitivity, always working with small groups. Bernbach would see anyone. His door was always open, and five

These posters marked the beginning of a campaign that made this authentic Jewish rye bread a delicacy appreciated far beyond the confines of New York.

115

chairs were always placed around his circular teak table for visitors. Almost all his colleagues called him

None of them were recruited using classical criteria. For Bernbach, advertising experience, age, gender, and educational qualifications were not really very important. Some of the agency's best employees had no experience in advertising. "I pull 'em in from all over the lot," he said. "And what there is to know about advertising, we teach them later." In the agency's early years, Bernbach was rarely in his office. He spent most of his time with the creative staff, going from one team to another, looking at work in progress. But he never imposed anything—he suggested. More than that, he questioned incessantly, thereby allowing the person he was talking to the pleasure and satisfaction of discovering a more intelligent approach, a better heading or design. All who worked with Bill agree that they became more mature and competent, without having to surrender their own personalities. Nevertheless, this new approach to

management

of an advertising agency, based on simplicity and informality, inevitably exposed those who lacked talent or were unmotivated. For the others, however, it provided real responsibility and the chance to use their abilities. As we shall see, all the best people who worked for DDB eventually became famous, whereas the colleagues of Lasker, Burnett, and, for the most part, Rubicam are forgotten. Bill Bernbach outlined a few principles, but he would never draw up a list of rules. When the AAAA published a study revealing that 85% of advertisements were ignored by the public, Bernbach wrote: "We can't question whether the public loves us. Business is spending its money for advertising and is achieving boredom with typical American efficiency." Rosser Reeves maintained that it sufficed to establish a single sales argument—the Unique Selling Proposition—and to repeat it as often as possible. Bernbach disagreed, declaring that the human mind gets bored with repetition and only reacts to different and new messages. "I am absolutely appalled," he said, "by the suggestion, indeed the policy, of some agencies that once the selling proposition has been determined the job is done." For Bernbach, carrying out numerous studies, attaching excessive importance to tests, and building the results of those tests up into certainties led ineluctably to uniformity and a failure to capture the viewer's interest. Bernbach felt that all advertisers commissioned the same types of studies, and obtained the same results, which were held to represent a sort of mathematical truth.

nd they all arrived at the same conclusions, resulting in the same type of standardized, sanitized, and inefficient advertisement. That did not mean that DDB did not have a research department, but it did not exert the same influence on campaigns as those of other agencies and, above all, it had no executive power. Power lay in the hands of Bernbach and what some called his "creative zoo." For Bernbach, the key thing was to follow your intuition and nourish those ideas that welled up from the unconscious when you were walking down the street or lying in bed. It was all about creating new things. Bernbach quoted a great jazz musician, Thelonius Monk, "Sometimes I play things I never heard myself." DDB never used brainstorming or group meetings. Campaigns were handled by teams made up of a graphic designer and a copywriter, who sat facing each other in the same office. This made it possible to create a fertile association where one idea could lead to a whole chain of further ideas. And there was no separation of tasks: the graphic designer was at liberty to come up with a heading and the copywriter could suggest a layout. It has to be said that this new approach to advertising and way of organizing work was not, in 1950, very reassuring for conventional clients, who were attached to the pseudo certainties

of science and frightened of the "wild" imaginations of creative people. As a result, DDB was unable to attract the biggest names in industry—there was no General Food account, no product of the Detroit automobile industry, no oil companies, no toothpaste brands, no soap or aspirin. The agency handled an airline, but it was El Al and not Pan Am; it had a bread manufacturer, but it was Levy's Rye and not Wonder; it had Barton candy and not Whitman. As for Ohrbach's, it was a large store only present in three cities, and Polaroid at the time was only a small company. Perhaps it was a good thing that DDB didn't have any big clients, because it enabled Bernbach to demonstrate his talent by propelling

almost unknown

brands to the heights of fame. A few years later, one of the biggest advertisers in America was looking for a new agency, so he summoned his managers and asked them to find out which agencies had done the campaigns for Polaroid, Volkswagen,

El Al, and Avis. Once the research had been completed, the choice was easy: the campaigns had all been done by DDB. It all began with Ohrbach's at the beginning of the 1950s. Bernbach had handled this account at Grey and it followed him to DDB in 1949. Since he had only a tiny budget for this small "big store," compared to the giant that they were sold as gifts in Macy's, Bernbach broke with the usual form of advertising for a business of this kind. He did not men-

The posters of the Polaroid campaign were so highly thought of that they were sold as gifts in Greenwich Village stores. Today, each one is worth a small fortune.

FIRST SHOWING OF A NEW POLAROID LAND FILM. This is an enlargement of an actual 60-second picture of Louis Armstrong. It was taken with a new film, just introduced, which is twice as sharp as the previous film.

With this latest development, the Polaroid Land Camera not only gives you pictures in 60 seconds, but pictures of exceptional clarity and brilliance. Polaroid Land Cameras start at $72.75. The new film can be identified by a star on the box.

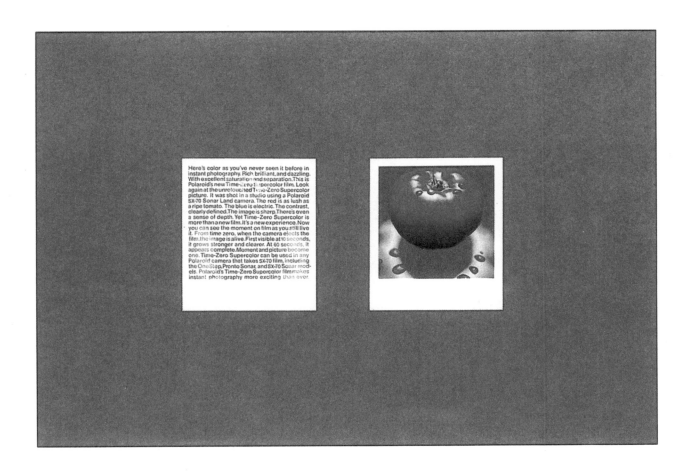

Here's color as you've never seen it before in instant photography. Rich, brilliant, and dazzling. With excellent saturation and separation. This is Polaroid's new Time-Zero Supercolor film. Look again at the unretouched Time-Zero Supercolor picture. It was shot in a studio using a Polaroid SX-70 Sonar Land camera. The red is as lush as a ripe tomato. The blue is electric. The contrast, clearly defined. The image is sharp. There's even a sense of depth. Yet Time-Zero Supercolor is more than a new film. It's a new experience. Now you can see the moment on film as you still live it. From time zero, when the camera ejects the film, the image is alive. First visible at 10 seconds, it grows stronger and clearer. At 60 seconds, it appears complete. Moment and picture become one. Time-Zero Supercolor can be used in any Polaroid camera that takes SX-70 film, including the One Step, Pronto Sonar, and SX-70 Sonar models. Polaroid's Time-Zero Supercolor film makes instant photography more exciting than ever.

tion prices of goods, focusing instead on creating a strong image of quality at afford-

A legendary product meets a leg-

able prices. All the advertisements that appeared in *The New York Times* have become

endary ad. The budget may have

part of legend and are the first examples of the characteristic Bernbach style: an intel-

been small, but the skillful cam-

ligent interplay of visuals and words using elements that attract attention but at the

paign more than made up for this.

same time say what there is to say. One of the very first advertisements for Ohrbach's showed a man going into a store with a woman under his arm. The heading read: "Liberal Trade-In: bring in your wife and just a few dollars . . . we will give you a new woman." DDB's Ohrbach's campaigns stimulated such sympathy and created such a bond with New Yorkers that it enabled Ohrbach's to challenge Macy's, even though the latter had thirty times more money to spend on advertising. But as Bernbach himself said: "It's not how often ads run," Bernbach explained, "it's how much excitement they create." Ohrbach's success quickly attracted another local advertiser, Henry S. Levy, an industrial bakery based in Brooklyn. They had a tiny budget of barely $40,000, but people were soon fighting over the ads for Levy's bread. The

The El Al campaign was one of
Bernbach's best known. It was
the first time that a campaign for
an airline omitted the pilot, air
hostesses, airplane, seats, and
food trays.

My son, the pilot.

by Tillie Katz

campaign showed different ethnic types, such as an Irish policeman, a Chinese laun-

dryman, and an Indian worker, and each one was devouring a rye bread sandwich.

The leitmotif of the whole campaign was: "You don't have to be Jewish to love Levy's

real Jewish rye." And Levy's Jewish rye bread became the most popular in New York.

In 1966, some fifteen years after the campaign, the posters were being sold in stores

in Greenwich Village.

t the time, DDB's territory was New York, or Manhattan to be

more precise. It was a local agency and Bernbach was king of the

Village. But the agency's reputation spread beyond the confines

of the city, because in 1954 it was entrusted with the Polaroid

account, still a relatively small company. Polaroid's system for taking instant photo-

graphs was, it has to be said, such a striking innovation that it made things easier for

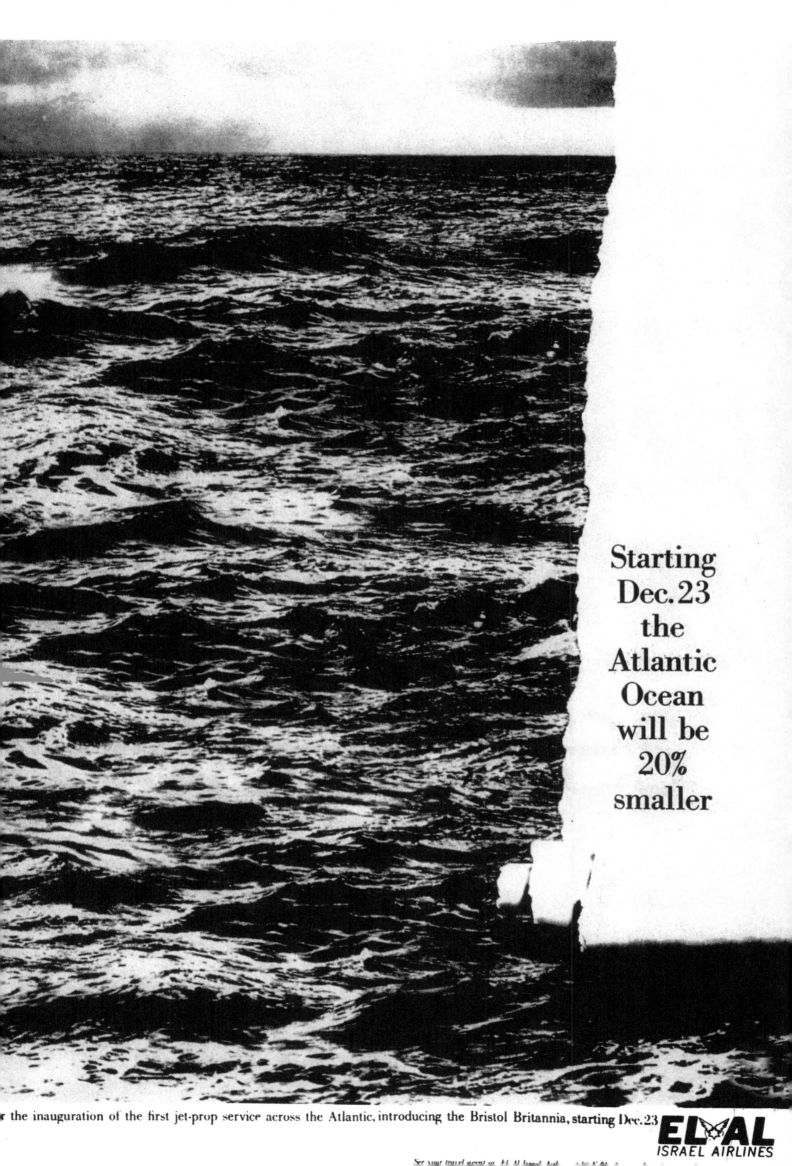

Starting
Dec. 23
the
Atlantic
Ocean
will be
20%
smaller

the inauguration of the first jet-prop service across the Atlantic, introducing the Bristol Britannia, starting Dec. 23

EL AL
ISRAEL AIRLINES

the agency. The launch took place on television with a one-minute film which had a very simple structure. It juxtaposed portraits of friends and families at the zoo, a wedding, a trip, each either smiling or crying thanks to Polaroid's instant photo. Polaroid's rise to fame was of course meteoric and the ads eventually appeared without headings and texts. Thus, in 1958, one ad simply showed a ridiculous little man on a beach holding a Polaroid camera in his hand, pursued by a horde of pin-ups. The airline El Al gave its account to DDB in 1957. At this time, advertising for airlines was a serious business and was governed by strict conventions. Ads always showed a single airplane on the page and the sea below was never shown on the pretext that people would be frightened that the plane would crash into it.

nce more, Bernbach ignored established rules. For the launch of the transatlantic New York-Tel Aviv flight, offering reduced prices of 20%, Bill had an ad created which showed a wild ocean, with the righthand part of the photo rolled up like a blind, and a heading saying: "Starting Dec. 23 the Atlantic Ocean will be 20% smaller." In subsequent ads, Bernbach continued to distance himself from the usual style adopted for airlines, producing one ad in particular that has remained famous. It shows an old lady sitting next to a framed photograph of a man in uniform. The heading reads: "My son, the pilot." The text recounts, in the voice of a Jewish mother, how her son had always been serious, intelligent, and well brought up, and how he had worked hard to become an El Al pilot. Within a year, El Al's revenue had tripled. The reputation of the campaigns produced by DDB continued to grow. From $8 million in 1954, the agency's business doubled within two years, passing the $20 million mark in 1957. In 1958, DDB won five of the eight gold medals awarded by the New York Art Directors Club. In its creative brio and rapid growth, DDB recalled the agency Young and Rubicam of the 1920s. Furthermore, Bill Bernbach bore a marked physical resemblance to Ray Rubicam. In the 1950s, DDB was neck and neck with

David Ogilvy's agency. Both agencies had become famous with small clients. In 1959, DDB became one of the top ten groups, with billings of $28 million, while Ogilvy, Benton & Mather had billings of $26 million, and Leo Burnett billings of $111 million. And yet none of these three most prominent agencies had a large national account. That did not seem to concern Bill Bernbach. For him, being one of the best agencies, or the best, was more important than being among the biggest. And yet, in 1959, ten years after the agency was founded, DDB continued to grow. Its new clients in that year included

volkswagen,

although the arrival of the German manufacturer was not greeted with joy in the agency. Firstly, they would be advertising a car without charm, without style, without power, and without an automatic transmission. Worse still, as the creator of the campaign Julian Koenig neatly put it, they would be "selling a Nazi car in the biggest Jewish city in the world!" Bernbach decided he would work directly on the account and asked Julian Koenig, the copywriter, to join him. Koenig refused point blank. He found it impossible to forget that Hitler himself had been directly involved in the Volkswagen project with the help of the Austrian engineer Ferdinand Porsche. For many people in 1959, and for Koenig in particular, who was Jewish, the sweet little Volkswagen still recalled the crematoria of the concentration camps. So Bernbach decided to get two other employees to work on Volkswagen: Helmut Krone and George Lois. Lois, who was Greek, refused, but Bernbach couldn't understand why. Then he discovered that several members of Lois's family had been massacred by the Germans and that his parents were only alive because a troop of resistance fighters had succeeded in halting the advance of a German column a few miles from their village. Bernbach protested that it was 1959 and times had changed, but Julian Koenig and George Lois would not be persuaded. So it was Helmut Krone alone

We're so confident of the new Polaroid 600 speed instant film and the new Polaroid Sun Cameras that we believe it's possible for you to get 10 good shots for 10 earnest tries every time. 10 for 10! The secret is in having the world's

10 good li

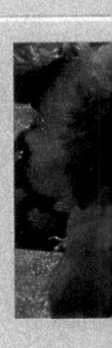

tle Indians.

who would team up with Bernbach to show Detroit that it was possible to challenge the big names with their colossal budgets with a

"nasty automobile"

and a tiny budget of $1 million. Helmut Krone was a first-generation German-American. He was obsessively methodical. Sober to the point of austerity, he was constantly hunched over his drawing board, never satisfied with the result. His recently acquired status as an American citizen meant that he was keen to do a campaign that was as American as possible. That seemed ridiculous to Bernbach, given the appearance of the Volkswagen. Faced with all the chrome, tail fins, and other adornments of American automobiles of the period, Bernbach thus decided that all the things that might appear as defects to the public should be turned into advantages. For example, the car's simple and utilitarian looks were due to the fact that it was cheap, and its underpowered engine meant it was more economical to run. When it came to putting this tricky approach into practice, Bernbach regretted that he did not have Julian Koenig to help him.

owever, by a stroke of luck, West Germany had just agreed to sell a fleet of fighter planes to Israel. Julian ran into Lois's office, and both agreed that the circumstances had changed. They went to see Bill Bernbach to tell him that they would work on the Volkswagen after all. Meanwhile, Helmut Krone had developed a type of layout for the campaign. Two-thirds of the surface would be devoted to the visual and one-third to the text, with the heading placed between the two. The visual was left in isolation, and the text was set in an austere sans serif typeface with blank spaces between paragraphs. All this gave the ads a strikingly simple look. Thirty years later, Volkswagen was still using this layout for its Beetle throughout the world. Bernbach decided to send Koenig and Lois to Wolfsburg, the Volkswagen

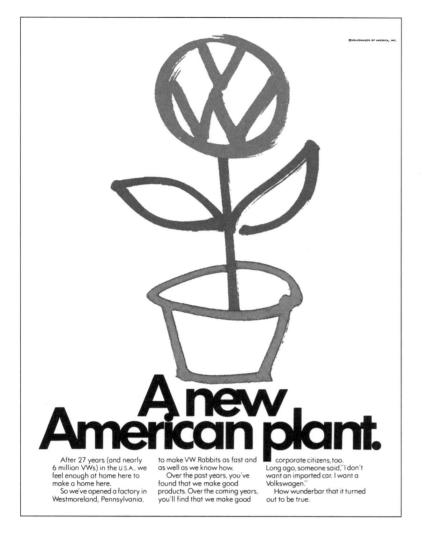

A new American plant.

After 27 years (and nearly 6 million VWs) in the U.S.A., we feel enough at home here to make a home here.

So we've opened a factory in Westmoreland, Pennsylvania,

to make VW Rabbits as fast and as well as we know how.

Over the past years, you've found that we make good products. Over the coming years, you'll find that we make good

corporate citizens, too.

Long ago, someone said, "I don't want an imported car. I want a Volkswagen."

How wunderbar that it turned out to be true.

Bernbach's most famous campaign was for Volkswagen—a staggering epic which began at the end of 1959 and lasted three decades.

headquarters. He sent a chaperon with them in the person of Ed McNeilly, head of advertising. Hardly had they arrived in Wolfsburg than Lois and Koenig went crazy. "Can you show us the ovens . . ." one of them asked the guide, while the other pointed out the slender form of a belltower to Dr. Nordhoff, the boss of Volkswagen, and added "It looks like a V2!" Dr. Nordhoff refused to talk to him again. And then they learned of a mysterious place where the earliest series of Volkswagens were kept, from the very first model, developed by Porsche, to the millionth, which was gold-plated. They nagged the people they were working with to see these historic models and were eventually taken into a deep basement where they found rows of automobiles covered in tarps. They were shown the first Volkswagen and then the millionth model. Lois asked to see the others but their hosts pretended not to hear him. Lois asked Koenig to keep everyone busy while he went up each row examining the tires of the concealed cars. Suddenly he spotted some models with larger cating an all-terrain model. He pulled aside the tarp to reveal a Volkswagen bearing

a swastika and fitted with a machine gun. Lois jumped into the vehicle and pointed

the machine gun at the group, which had its back to him, and began to shout "Ach!

Ach! Ach!" Julian Koenig jumped into the seat next to him and, parodying

Goebbels, made the "Heil Hitler" salute. Poor Ed McNeilly, the chaperon, went as

white as a sheet and shrunk back against the wall. Eventually the team returned to

DDB without having lost the client and started work. The first Volkswagen ad to

come out in the layout designed by Helmut Krone bore the heading "Think Small."

This was followed by: "Ten years ago, the first Volkswagens were imported into the

United States. These strange little cars with their

beetle

shapes were almost unknown. All they had to recommend them was 32 miles to the gallon (regular gas, regular driving), an aluminum air-cooled rear engine that would go 70 mph all day without strain, sensible size for a family and a sensible price tag." Another of the ads had the heading "Lemon," and the text: "This Volkswagen missed the boat. The chrome strip on the glove compartment is blemished and

Lemon.

This Volkswagen missed the boat.
The chrome strip on the glove compartment is blemished and must be replaced. Chances are you wouldn't have noticed it; Inspector Kurt Kroner did.
There are 3,389 men at our Wolfsburg factory with only one job: to inspect Volkswagens at each stage of production. (3000 Volkswagens are produced daily; there are more inspectors

than cars.)
Every shock absorber is tested (spot checking won't do), every windshield is scanned. VWs have been rejected for surface scratches barely visible to the eye.
Final inspection is really something! VW inspectors run each car off the line onto the Funktionsprüfstand (car test stand), tote up 189 check points, gun ahead to the automatic

brake stand, and say "no" to one VW out of fifty.
This preoccupation with detail means the VW lasts longer and requires less maintenance, by and large, than other cars. (It also means a used VW depreciates less than any other car.)
We pluck the lemons; you get the plums.

128

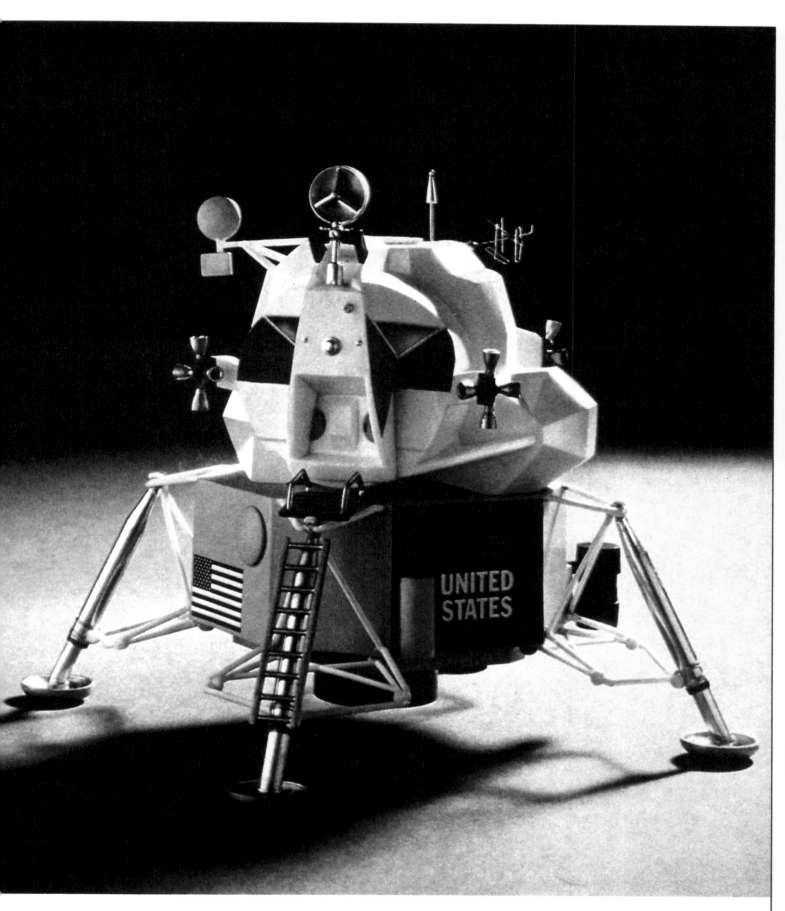

It's ugly, but it gets you there.

must be replaced. . . . We pluck the lemons; you get

the plums." The creative teams changed, but the style,

the tone, and the humor remained the same through-

out the various VW ads. At the beginning of 1962, a full-page ad appeared showing

a small VW above the title "Don't forget the anti-

freeze!" There was also the contented country hick

pictured in front of his new VW, above the heading

"It was the only thing to do after the mule died!"

Later, when American astronauts were setting foot on the moon, DDB created an ad

showing the lunar module, with the heading: "It's

ugly, but it gets you there." The television ads adopt-

ed a similar pithy approach. One of the earliest of

these, shot in black and white, shows a VW in a snowy

landscape driving up to a hangar. The voiceover says: "Have you ever wondered

how the man who drives the snowplow drives to the

snowplow? . . . This one drives a Volkswagen. . . . So

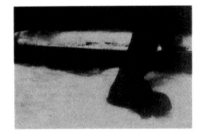

you can stop wondering." The VW campaigns proved

so effective that the public overlooked the car's small-

ness and poor safety. People who had worked on the VW ads were treated on

Madison Avenue as if they had written a bestseller.

The VW campaigns mesmerized the advertising

The American public lapped up

world and had a far-reaching influence. Agencies and

DDB's ads and commercials for

advertisers all demanded campaigns in a similar style.

Volkswagen. The Beetle, the small

Long after, in 1976, when the trade magazine *Advertising Age* asked its readers to pick

car that the snowplow driver uses

the best advertisements they had ever seen, 60% of

to fetch his snowplow, was a star

them picked VW campaigns. In the wake of this suc-

in New York.

cess, in the autumn of 1962, the rental car company

The original Beetle is dead, but the humor of the ads lives on, even if not everyone today is as talented as Julian Koenig.

The green fender came
   off a '58.
The blue hood came
   off a '59.
The beige fender came
   off a '64.
The turquoise door came
   off a '62.
Most VW parts
   are interchangeable
   from one year to the next.
That's why parts
   are so easy to get.

Avis switched its $1.5 million account from McCann-Erickson to DDB. This also proved to be a problematic account, another poisoned gift. Avis was losing money and was being trumped by Hertz. Once again, Bernbach used the technique of turning a weakness into a strength, adopting the same tone as that used in the VW ads: "Avis is only No. 2 in rent a cars. So why go with us?" The answer was: "We try harder." Many advertisers would have thrown this type of advertising back at their agency. Indeed, a preliminary test carried out with a consumer panel had produced poor results. According to the analysts, Americans generally only put their trust in winners. Once again, Bernbach paid no heed to this. Avis's share of the market increased by 28%, with billings rising from $3.5 million to $5 million. The campaign continued to evolve, but always on the same theme, cruelly targeting the number one, Hertz. Avis's slogan, "We try harder" was on everyone's lips and even appeared on lapel badges which were sold to the public. The success of Volkswagen and Avis prompted other big advertisers to join DDB. It had taken fourteen years. American Airlines and Seagram (the largest alcoholic drinks group in the world) arrived from Young and Rubicam. They were followed by Heinz, Sony, Uniroyal, Lever, Gillette, Bristol Myers, and Mobil. In 1966, DDB joined the club of top ten agencies in the world, with billings of $130 million. But what pleased Bill more was to be chosen as the best in opinion polls. For, despite the success and wealth, Bill Bernbach had not really changed.

ow that his children had grown up, he left the house in Brooklyn for an apartment in the UN Plaza in the center of Manhattan. But he was still attached to his past. To the great displeasure of the trendy creative people in the agency, on the radiator in his office stood a doe and fawns made of spun glass. These kitsch objects were a souvenir from his childhood in Brooklyn. He still looked like an accountant or a history professor, although he now occasionally dared to sport stripes or spots on his tie. He devoted all his time to advertising and its practitioners. Indeed, for them he was the "prophet," and they were his disciples. Going to see him was like having an audience.

Having lunch with him was an event. "Did you lunch with Bill? What did he talk about? What did he say? What did you say to him?" If you answered by saying that you talked about nothing in particular and that Bill ate a tuna sandwich, everyone would look disappointed. To satisfy the disciples, it would perhaps have been better to answer that a blind man had come up to the table, that Bill had blessed him, and that the blind man had left the restaurant with 20-20 vision in each eye! People were not afraid of Bernbach, and Bill's

"creative zoo"

was made up of talented people with strong personalities. They included the three greatest graphic designers of the time: Paul Rand, Bob Gage, and Helmut Krone. And then there was Phyllis Robinson, who was head of copywriting and had several young women under her wing, notably Judy Protas, Paula Green, and Mary Wells

I'll be home for Chivas.

Put your hand over the gray half and see how much younger I lo

(DDB also differed from other agencies in that it employed a higher number of women). Other distinguished people who worked at DDB included Ed Vellanti, David Herzourn, John Noble, Ron Rosenfeld, a future copywriting star, and the unruly Julian Koenig, already a star, who was the most gifted of all. Koenig would spend the day at the racetrack and wrote his best-known ads in one hour, which exasperated Helmut

Avis is only No.2 in rent a cars. So why go with us?

We try harder.
(When you're not the biggest, you have to.)
We just can't afford dirty ashtrays. Or half-empty gas tanks. Or worn wipers. Or unwashed cars. Or low tires. Or anything less than seat-adjusters that adjust. Heaters that heat. Defrosters that defrost.
Obviously, the thing we try hardest for is just to be nice. To start you out right with a new car, like a lively, super-torque Ford, and a pleasant smile. To know, say, where you get a good pastrami sandwich in Duluth.
Why?
Because we can't afford to take you for granted.
Go with us next time.
The line at our counter is shorter.

Krone, a fierce believer in talent through sweat. There was also the rather unrefined George Lois, who would also be much talked about. When they left DDB, Bill's disciples would preach the Bernbach creative creed. Some joined other agencies; others set up their own businesses. Some were unable to succeed outside of DDB, and eventually came back to their "dad." For its own publicity, DDB once even used a letter from a copywriter sent to Bill. This copywriter explained that he had been unhappy since he had left and that he wished to come back to DDB. The disciples of the great Bill would give American advertising a new lease on life. Bill initiated a creative revolution that would spread to other agencies, a revolution that would make some, notably Mary Wells, Julian Koenig, and George Lois, famous and wealthy. In 1964, DDB was floated on the New York stock market. The idea had been Max Dane's, with the aim of getting funds to enable the agency to diversify. Bill Bernbach allowed it to happen, but it is clear that this quest for diversification and internationalization did not interest him. Bill wanted to be the king of Manhattan—London, Paris, and even Los Angeles left him indifferent. He wanted DDB to be the best advertising agency, without any dilution of quality. Subsequent

This visual for Clairol serves as a superb, if surreal, demonstration of the product's efficiency. The equally superb campaign for Avis consisted of claiming that a company does more for its clients when it is only number two.

events seemed to prove him right. With the agency's introduction on the stock market, diversification, and the creation of a network of offices, DDB seemed to lose its uniqueness, its strength, and its soul. Unlike other agencies, DDB was a chapel, built by one man: Bill Bernbach. And unlike Volkswagen Beetles, Bernbachs could not be mass-produced. As we have seen, his best disciples set up on their own. Furthermore, Bernbach's approach, when it was misunderstood or misinterpreted, gave rise to trendy young creative people who were more interested in advertising for itself than for the sales results achieved by the clients. At the beginning of the 1970s, Bernbach warned the profession against the development of what Rosser Reeves called the

narcissists

of advertising. These new members of the profession had completely forgotten that

their role was to make the product interesting. After ten years of creative supremacy and stunning commercial results, DDB began the 1970s by losing one of its biggest accounts: Alka-Seltzer. The client criticized the agency not because it made films that entertained or made people laugh, but because fewer people were buying the product. Alka-Seltzer's share of the market was shrinking, so it was goodbye DDB. The $20 million went instead to Wells, Rich, Greene, a new agency created by Mary Wells, one of the great Bill's former disciples. The bad run continued for DDB—Lever, Whirlpool, Sara Lee, Quaker Oats, Cracker Jack, and a few others left the agency. As a result, business had dropped by $33 million in 1972. In 1973, the agency lost a further $11 million in accounts. These losses were in part compensated for by the acquisition of small agencies and the development of an international network. But Rome was not Rome any more and DDB was no longer DDB. And Bill, now nearly sixty-three, was alone. He who had always prided himself on hiring carefully, training brilliantly, never firing anyone, and maintaining an exciting work atmosphere now saw DDB in a seriously unstable position, torn by conflict, buffeted by managers coming and going, a victim of passing advertising fashions. It was incredible. DDB was becoming a run-of-the-mill agency like any other. Worse still, the regular loss of accounts gave them a reputation as losers, leading to further losses. The scent of blood drew the sharks. "Get DDB!" became the watchword on Madison Avenue.

Unlike the El Al campaign, there was an airplane in this ad for American Airlines.

Fame ha

"Doctor, it's gotten to the point where people are constantly asking for my autograph. I can't even eat my chorizos in peace."

These words recently came from the fatigued form of Juan Valdez. Along w his partner he's starting to feel the pressure of success.

The cause of it all, of course, is their huge television exposure for Colombi Coffee. In fact this year alone, Juan and his friend will be seen almost 2 billio times in American living rooms.

ts price.

Frankly they've proven to be successful spokesmen. A recent survey indicates
that most Americans now believe that Colombian Coffee is the best in the world.
Which, unfortunately for Juan, makes him even more popular.

What this means to you is that if you're not offering a 100% Colombian Coffee
brand, it's time to start. Every day you delay you're losing potential profits.

And if you let that happen you'll end up like Juan. Spilling the beans to a
psychiatrist.   The National Federation of Coffee Growers of Colombia 140 East 57th Street New York, N Y 10022

100% Colombian Coffee

n fact, DDB's Achilles' heel was also the element that had made it the greatest of agencies: Bill himself. For although Bill was unquestionably the best when it came to new concepts, creativity, talent, and innovation, he was also independent and solitary, proud but lacking ambition, hungry for success but not ruthless. He was not a smart businessman like Leo Burnett or David Ogilvy, who saw their enterprises survive them and prosper. The creation of an international network, the opening of branches, acquisitions, mergers, solid billings—none of these things interested Bernbach. He liked the products more than the clients, the advertising message more than phoney science. Outside of DDB in New York there could be no DDB, because there was no Bill. When Bill died on October 2, 1982, there would still be a little of Bernbach in other agencies where his disciples were working, but there would never be another DDB. It was all very well pinning up the sayings of the great Bill on the walls of the agencies: the magician was no longer there and the magic had gone with him. After many changes, without Doyle, Dane, and Bernbach among others, DDB merged with Needham, Harper and Steers under the control of the Saatchi Brothers. But the campaigns for Levy's, Ohrbach's, Volkswagen, Polaroid, Alka-Seltzer, and Sony are eternal. That is Bill's legacy.

New watches arrive on the market:

thanks to DDB, the Bulova

Accutron was the most famous

and commercially successful

watch for a long time.

EQUAL PAY. EQUAL TIME.

BULOVA ACCUTRON®
For men and women.

Both watches are equally accurate to within a minute a month.* Hers is #24901. His #23700. Each one is $175.
*Timekeeping will be adjusted to this tolerance, if necessary, if returned to Accutron dealer from whom purchased within one year from date of purchase.

DO THIS OR DIE.

Is this ad some kind of trick?

No. But it could have been.

And at exactly that point rests a do or die decision for American business.

We in advertising, together with our clients, have all the power and skill to trick people. Or so we think.

But we're wrong. We can't fool *any* of the people *any* of the time.

There is indeed a twelve-year-old mentality in this country; every six-year-old has one.

We are a nation of smart people.

And most smart people ignore most advertising because most advertising ignores smart people.

Instead we talk to each other.

We debate endlessly about the medium and the message. Nonsense. In advertising, the message *itself* is the message.

A blank page and a blank television screen are one and the same.

And above all, the messages we put on those pages and on those television screens must be the truth. For if we play tricks with the truth, we die.

Now. The other side of the coin.

Telling the truth about a product demands a product that's worth telling the truth *about.*

Sadly, so many products aren't.

So many products don't do anything better. Or anything different. So many don't work quite right. Or don't last. Or simply don't matter.

If we also play this trick, we also die. Because advertising only helps a bad product fail faster.

No donkey chases the carrot forever. He catches on. And quits.

That's the lesson to remember.

Unless we do, we die.

Unless we change, the tidal wave of consumer indifference will wallop into the mountain of advertising and manufacturing drivel.

That day we die.

We'll die in *our* marketplace. On *our* shelves. In *our* gleaming packages of empty promises.

Not with a bang. Not with a whimper.

But by our own skilled hands.

DOYLE DANE BERNBACH INC.